how to expect
what you're
not expecting

how to expect what you're not expecting

STORIES OF PREGNANCY PARENTHOOD AND LOSS

EDITED BY **JESSICA HIEMSTRA**
AND **LISA MARTIN-DEMOOR**

FOREWORD BY **KIM JERNIGAN**

TouchWood
Editions

TouchWood Editions
touchwoodeditions.com

LIBRARY AND ARCHIVES CANADA CATALOGUING IN PUBLICATION
How to expect what you're not expecting : stories of pregnancy, parenthood and loss / edited by Jessica Hiemstra and Lisa Martin-DeMoor.

Issued also in electronic formats.
ISBN 978-1-77151-021-9

1. Miscarriage. 2. Infertility. 3. Stillbirth. 4. Loss (Psychology). 5. Pregnancy. 6. Parenthood. I. Hiemstra, Jessica, 1979– II. Martin-DeMoor, Lisa, 1979– III. Title: How to expect what you are not expecting.

RG648.H69 2013   155.9'37   C2013-902068-3

Proofreader: Sarah Weber, Lightning Editorial
Design: Pete Kohut
Cover image: Shawna Lemay
Interior illustrations: Jessica Hiemstra

We gratefully acknowledge the financial support for our publishing activities from the Government of Canada through the Canada Book Fund, Canada Council for the Arts, and the province of British Columbia through the British Columbia Arts Council and the Book Publishing Tax Credit.

MIX
Paper from responsible sources
FSC® C016245

The interior pages of this book have been printed on 30% post-consumer recycled paper, processed chlorine free, and printed with vegetable-based inks.

1 2 3 4 5 17 16 15 14 13

PRINTED IN CANADA

To everyone with a story like
this to tell: this book is for you.

contents

Navigating Loss

KIM JERNIGAN

> Born in a time
> of darkness, you will learn the trick of making.
> You shall make your consolation all your life.
> —Amanda Jernigan, "Lullaby"†

THIS BOOK, THE ONE you hold in your hands, this book about loss and longing and the half-life of grief, is a wonderful book, one you will want to read, and read again, and share with someone dear to you. This might be a surprise, or at least it was to me, for it's a book in large part about the greatest of heartaches, the loss of a child. And yet the book is more than that, as the careful grouping of these essays suggests. It's about unexpected and inescapable loss (What You Have Is What Happened), yes, but it's also about hope (The Wounded Past Cannot Deny the Beautiful Future), about the search for meaning (The Desire to Understand), and about love (The Possibility of Love). It's also about making.

The book's title, *How to Expect What You're Not Expecting*, a play on the title of the popular pregnancy and childbirth manual *What to*

Expect When You're Expecting, presents a conundrum (there is, after all, no way to expect the unexpected) but also a way of reading the essays as a whole. "What to Expect" implies something straightforward and normative; "How to Expect" *can* suggest something prescriptive, but also, as here, something various: there are as many "hows" as there are individuals and circumstances.

A litany of the losses covered here includes infertility, miscarriage, accidental pregnancy, stillbirths, premature births, the birth of a child with a debilitating physical or neurological problem, the giving up of a child to adoption, the loss of an adolescent to drugs or despair, the after effects of childhood abuse on one's own parenting, the problem of parental guilt, and of our inability to protect our children not only from the world but from themselves. Yet this stark list suggests little of the essays on the page, each an account not of a condition but of a full, rich, familiar life. Familiar because even those of us for whom the arrival of children was joyfully uncomplicated register that a birth moves one up in the mortal queue and foretells, if it doesn't coincide with, the loss of one's parents.

Yet threaded through this sadness and the effort to find solace, or at least to cope, is also a host of other topics: the history of dolls, robots, automata, and miniatures as fetish objects (Cathy Stonehouse); the perils of finding love oceans away from friends and family and a familiar health care system (Erika Connor); the attractions of magical thinking, of dreams and portents and good luck charms (various); the difference the Internet makes "not only in the medical outcomes of pregnancy . . . but also in shaping our understanding of the physical process, which in turn shapes how we feel" (Laura Rock); chaos theory (Kevin Bray); the consolations of painting or poetry (Jessica Hiemstra, Yvonne Blomer); ancient Danish and Egyptian burial rites (Chris Arthur).

The book's editors, Jessica Hiemstra and Lisa Martin-DeMoor, call this "the ecology of loss": the way those who've suffered a loss tend to shape their emotional response in terms of their occupations and avocations. The very first essay, Chris Tarry's "Largo, Lento, Grave"—the musical terms for "broadly," "slowly," "slow and solemn"—is a case in point. It's the story of a baby, long in the conceiving, who withers in the womb. It's written by that baby's father, a musician, who connects viscerally to his child's declining heartbeat and finds in it something he knows and understands, the idea of tempo, that aspect of musical composition that affects the mood and difficulty of a piece.

It's a commonplace that grief diminishes over time, but I've always found it more comforting to think of it as something that goes deeper, not something that will forever dog your days but something that is accessible, that will be triggered by certain memories or melodies, sounds or smells, places or times of year. Being able to access one's grief is a way of keeping a loved one present and in the world, as music will do for this father. Tarry also gives one of the best answers I've ever heard to the question of when life begins: "The best that I can figure is that it starts in the heart, and grows from there." You know from this essay onward that you are in good hands, that the language will lift you even when the subject distresses.

And yet these writers (all of the essayists are writers, visual artists, or musicians as well as parents, actual or hopeful) have a complex and freighted connection to language. As Chris Arthur, whose essay "Swan Song" is one of the most circumspect, artful, and yet unexpectedly moving in the collection, says, "where the subject lies close-quartered with the heart, getting words to work is hard. Such proximity makes them prey to so many meltdowns—into cliché, melodrama, exaggeration, pathos, sentimentality—that it's tempting to lapse into silence and say nothing, or rest content with the roughest of approximations." Add to that the concern that certain sorrows "seem improper to disclose, seem to warrant discretion, not description."

"Mutual silence," Maureen Scott Harris suggests in her essay "Opening the Griefcase," can also be "a strategy to keep us safe and at a distance from each other's hurts." Contrary impulses war in her as she attempts to tell her story: "I want to find the line of continuity between now and then, making a map through time. But again and again I find myself where words fail me and the line is broken, the map left blank."

So begins, here and throughout the collection, a casting about for narrative strategies that will allow the writer's story to be told. Collage is one of them, the breaking of a story into sections in the hope that somehow they will convey a certain truth to feeling, collectively or in the spaces between them. Word play is another, exposing the ways in which language is prejudicial or falls short of experience: "Miscarry: like carrying the ball forward and fumbling it. Like mistake. Like miscarriage of justice" (Laura Rock). Or the section headings in Susan Olding's essay on infertility, each of them a different take on the word "barren." Or Cathy Stonehouse noting how the word "lost" feels weird in the context of a sentence like "I lost my first child, a daughter, after five months in utero." Other writers reach for metaphor, searching out, or happening upon, clarifying similarities, as between a dropped egg and a lost fetus: "And there, across the table where my fried egg lay critically wounded, I saw the most basic choice I believe we make in this world: who to blame, who to hold responsible" (Lisa Martin-DeMoor).

Narrative reversals also abound: telling the story backwards as a way of emphasizing how loss recasts everything that came before (Gail Marlene Schwartz, Janet Baker). Or avoiding endings entirely as Jennifer Bowering Delisle does, her closing scene a still-life of husband and wife at the kitchen table trying to decide whether to "cook" or "bake" a child—whether to have one naturally, or not at all, or to resort to intrauterine insemination. They've reached this stasis because, whatever they decide, the outcome is uncertain.

The necessity of giving over the illusion of control is, in fact, the overarching theme of the book, played out as thesis and antithesis: "How strong the need was to control my own life, every moment, every breath of it. How deep my faith that such a thing was possible" (Olding). "I saw myself as a proactive decision maker, giving informed consent, taking control. Now I realize that data have limits; the body follows its course whether or not the monitors are turned on" (Rock). "I have learned through experience and theory that much of life is too complex to be foretold, that predictions are intemperate" (Bray). Even Carrie Snyder's essay, the aptly titled "Delivery," which ends the gathering and in which she attempts to deliver herself from an accumulation of sorrows, reminds us that "We none of us can guess the effects, the ripples that pool outward and spread and rock our lives, and change us . . . there is only ever the illusion of conclusion, of ending. We hold because we grieve. We grieve because we love. And we wait in the possibility of love without grief. We wait as best we can."

They wait . . . and they write. Writing is an attempt to control what they can, to frame, shape, or, in the language of psychologists, to "restory" their loss. To accept the impossibility of turning back the clock, of changing the outcome, and instead change what they *make* of what has happened. They write, then, for their own sakes, seeking the release that comes from imposing a shape on raw experience. "[T]he years after a loss change its meaning. Memories shift, rearranging themselves into a new order" (Rock).

But, like all writers who cast their words upon the waters hoping they'll wash up on a welcoming shore, they also write for a reader. As one of the first readers this book has had, I asked myself what comfort I might take from their stories, what wisdom. I suspect that word "wisdom" might make these writers squirm. While there may be much we can take away in terms of understanding and insight, it is not the writers' *intention* to advise or instruct. If they give advice it's mostly of the cautionary sort ("Expect anything"). The purpose of these essays, of writing them and of publishing them together in this way, is less to provide an answer than to provide an example, less to inform than to explore, to share a story, or stories, that might have wider resonance. And yet I did feel comforted as I read, more than comforted. I felt happy to be alive and in such company.

We all belong to the country of the bereaved. Even those of us who have so far weathered parenthood without major loss have suffered what Stonehouse calls "the constant loss, the tiny griefs as each stage of childhood finishes, even as what replaces [it] grows more profound." We want our children to be independent, yet we worry about them as they go out into the world and are buffeted by it. Love makes us vulnerable. Together these writers give us "a glimpse of how the heart and the imagination may work together to transform and transcend death" (Fiona Tinwei Lam). They show us how to embrace the rituals of remembrance, how to make something, to give something, to enter one's own pain or someone else's. And they do it in language that is often itself transcendent. Beauty, they caution, is a poor substitute for a life cut short. But to say that the essays here are beautiful doesn't necessarily mean that the writing is lyrical or sonorous or highly wrought—though it's sometimes that—only (only!) that it has captured something nuanced, has found the words and the structures of meaning that collapse the distance between what is said and what is understood.

Beauty is the balm sought by both editors of this collection, and beauty is the gift they give us. As Jessica Hiemstra puts it, "Beauty might not be necessary, but we need it."

KIM JERNIGAN studied American literature at Bryn Mawr College in the United States and Canadian literature at the University of Waterloo in Canada, where she has devoted thirty-plus years to editing *The New Quarterly*, a magazine of contemporary Canadian poetry, fiction, and essays.

†Lines taken from "Lullaby" from *All the Daylight Hours*, by Amanda Jernigan, published by Cormorant Books Inc. Copyright © 2013 Amanda Jernigan. Used by permission of the publisher.

how to
expect

WHAT YOU HAVE
IS WHAT HAPPENED

Largo, Lento, Grave

CHRIS TARRY

ACCELERANDO

(quickly, and with excitement)

My wife Michelle and I decided to have a baby while driving home from a late-night party in New Jersey. We'd spent the evening cooing over a friend's slightly bizarre-looking three-week-old. "Do they always look like aliens?" I asked.

"They come cuter than that," Michelle said.

"I want seventy-five percent cuter," I said. We talked like that in those days. Like we could order a baby from the back of the *New Yorker*.

It was June 2009 and we'd been married three years. Michelle worked for a large clothing manufacturer in their legal department, and I was a working musician—constantly on the road. Along with work, Michelle had gone back to school part-time for a master's degree in international economics, and she was nearly finished. She'd suffered through three years of executive work hours and 10:00 PM classes and was in the middle of her thesis. The stress level was high.

"I want to make you the only pregnant girl in class," I told her as we pointed the Subaru over the George Washington Bridge toward Brooklyn. She rolled her eyes at me and looked out the window. "You do, do ya?"

"I think we're ready," I said, gripping the steering wheel a little tighter. I looked over. Michelle was deep in thought. She's a quiet thinker. I love that about her.

On the FDR we discussed the baby's timing—this was New York after all, the kid needed to be on a schedule. On the Williamsburg Bridge we talked about the colour of the baby's room, green it was decided. On the Brooklyn Queens Expressway we came up with names, Zachary for a boy, Chloe if it was a girl. By the time we'd parked the car outside our Brooklyn apartment, the decision was made. Michelle leaned over and kissed me. "Let's get to it," she said. And we did.

CESURA
(break, stop. i.e., a complete break in sound)
And we did. And we did. And we did. And a year later, still no baby.

If someone had told me how hard it was to get pregnant, I would have stopped buying condoms in my twenties. For me, babies had always meant preventative measures. Take away the prevention, add the thrill of something akin to jumping out of a plane without a parachute, and bam, instant baby.

My understanding of the human reproductive system jumped tenfold that year. I became an expert in all things sperm-and-egg. I'd catch myself on gigs telling drummers about ovulation cycles and the latest detection equipment.

"They make this new thing," I'd tell them. "It'll track your wife's cycle and let you know when it's the best time to have sex."

"Sounds romantic," they'd say.

I became a fathering machine. If the chart said four o'clock on a Wednesday was the best time for sex, I'd be standing next to the bed naked by three forty-five. If someone told me too much garlic was bad for sperm production, I'd eat dry noodles for a month. Michelle became an expert in prenatal vitamins. Folic acid in the mornings, iron and calcium at night. There was prenatal yoga, prenatal spin class, prenatal Pilates, and a book called *What to Expect When You're Expecting*. Michelle didn't drink for a year.

And with all of it, the ever-present thesis. School became a ball of stress that attached itself to my wife every night and wouldn't let go. After a year of dry pasta, vitamins, scheduled sex, and the thesis, we were exhausted. Michelle was convinced there was something wrong.

CON ANIMA
(with feeling)

The Internet was telling me that tight underwear killed sperm and I'd been a briefs man my whole life. The "something wrong" was obviously me.

"You'd be amazed," said Dr. Vapnek. "By the time most guys are sitting in my office, their wives are already pregnant." My urologist told me this while writing out a referral to a semen analysis clinic. "There's something about making the decision to get tested that frees the mind," he said. "It reduces the stress. Trust me, you'll see. I've been doing this a very long time."

He sent me over to a building that looked like a day spa. There was soft music, and an attractive receptionist who had me fill out forms. There were questions like, When was the last time you had sex? How often do you masturbate? Have you masturbated in the past five days? *Like I had time for that*, I said to myself, and thought longingly back to my teenage years when masturbation was pretty much the focus of my day. I brought the forms to the desk.

She led me to a room with a huge armchair in the middle and a big-screen TV on the wall. There were porn magazines spread out on a coffee table from the eighties. She told me to take the sample to the office down the hall when I was finished, and excused herself.

I walked around the room checking out the plants. I looked out the window that faced Sixth Avenue and watched the hundreds of people streaming toward midtown. I sat in the big chair and stared at the ceiling. I spent a few minutes fiddling with the TV and gave up. I thumbed through *Asian Babes* and *Celebrity Skin*. It was three in the afternoon and I wondered how many guys had been in that room and done what I was about to do.

I was out of practice. I needed my own apartment. Get me in that room when I was seventeen and I would have walked out with some smart ass comment like, "Here ya go everyone, there's plenty more where that came from." But it was different now. I had a routine and this was the furthest thing from it. I looked at the cup. What kind of aim did they expect, exactly? It felt like one of those midway games where you try to swish the basketball only to discover that they've made the hoop so small you can't win.

I'm not sure what level of masculinity is wrapped up in the volume of one's own semen sample sitting at the bottom of a plastic cup, but let's just say my ego was severely crushed that day. *There's no way something like that could get anyone pregnant*, I thought as I stood in the middle of the room looking down at my less than adequate handiwork. I sheepishly brought the sample down the hall and set it on the counter.

It's my fault, I said to myself as I walked out onto Sixth Avenue. *I'm the problem.*

Three weeks later, Michelle was pregnant.

GUSTOSO
(with happy emphasis)
I got the phone call while walking down Queen Street in Toronto. I was playing two nights at a local jazz club. Michelle was so excited I thought she was going to jump through the phone. I stopped in the middle of the street and did this kind of movie move, that thing where you look up into the sky and spin around a few times. Before she'd called I'd been taking stock of everyone that walked by and wondering how they'd all been born. How were so many people walking around in

the world when it was this hard to get pregnant? And then the phone call, and the elation, and good God, it was finally happening to us. "I'm going to be a dad!" I yelled to anyone on the street who would listen. A few people looked at me like they were about to be mugged.

I got back to the hotel and texted the band. Then I phoned my parents. Then my brothers. Then anyone on the West Coast who wouldn't mind being woken up with the kind of news I was packing. Then I went for another walk. Everything looked different. The buildings were somehow taller, people were smiling more, the sky was clearer. I'd never been that happy.

Michelle and I talked on the phone nearly twenty times that day. We attempted to pinpoint the moment of conception, the precise timing of it all.

"I think it was when we tried that special position from the book," I told her.

"Could be," she said. "Practically needed a spotter for that one." We both laughed and she cried and I told her what a wonderful moment this was. The line went silent for a long while.

"I wish you were here," Michelle said eventually.

"Me too," I said. "When's the doctor's appointment?"

"Tomorrow," she said.

Tomorrow meant that I'd be flying home from Toronto and be back in Brooklyn before Michelle returned from work, and classes, and a meeting with her thesis advisor. It was eleven o'clock at night before she walked through the door, twenty-four hours after she'd told me the news. She looked tired.

"What did the doctor say?" I jumped from the couch and muted the TV. I gave her the longest hug.

"We're pregnant," she said.

Jon Stewart was on. I unmuted the TV. "Perfect," she said, smiling at her favourite show. She pulled off her shoes, curled up on the couch, and fell asleep.

AD LIBITUM

(the speed and manner of execution are left to the performer)

Over the next four weeks I Googled everything I could on the first six weeks of pregnancy. I bookmarked pictures of various amorphous blobs and pulled them out in the evenings when Michelle needed a break from the thesis work. "Look, arm buds!" I'd say, pointing to a picture. "I think we're about this stage."

"I hope it gets cuter," she'd say.

Michelle worked in Times Square, which made it easy to get to the doctor's office on her lunch break. Just a quick trip on the A train to Lincoln Center. For the sixth-week appointment I took the train in from Brooklyn and met her at Dr. Francis's office. I remember how I felt on the subway ride over, like I wanted to get up and hug everyone on the train. It was the day we were going to finally see our munchkin on the monitor. Michelle had taken a long lunch. "Everyone in the office is so excited," she told me when I met her outside the clinic.

We sat in a pale green examination room waiting for the doctor, Michelle was already in the stirrups, the nurse had come in, taken her blood, and given her a gown. We both sat nervously discussing work, gigs, the thesis, anything but baby.

Dr. Francis carried herself with a calming ease. "I always love it when the husbands show up to the early appointments," she said as she walked in and shook my hand. "You guys ready to see your baby?" I held Michelle's hand and we nodded at the same time.

The monitor bleeped to life and Dr. Francis moved Michelle into position. She put gel on a long probe and I thought, *Jesus, that doesn't look comfortable!* On the monitor there was a lot of black and white nothingness that seemed to move by very quickly. Dr. Francis talked calmly to us about the weather, her kids, and Brooklyn. She moved the probe around inside Michelle until a black patch slowly came into view on the screen, and then a small dot of something unrecognizable. She zoomed in, rotated the picture, and froze the image. "There you go," she said. "There's your baby."

Michelle and I looked at each other, it looked like a pixilated eighties computer game character. Dr. Francis looked up and saw that Michelle was crying. "I hope that's a happy cry?" she said in the softest doctor voice ever.

"It took so long," Michelle said. "I can't believe it's really happening."

"Oh, it's happening," said Dr. Francis, and we all laughed.

The doctor snapped a picture and took a few measurements. "Computer is telling me you're six weeks and two days," she said. "When was conception?" We laughed again, Michelle and I were a little embarrassed. We'd had so much sex that pinning down a specific date was like finding a needle in the haystack we'd spent the year rolling in. We weren't quite sure, we told her.

"No worries," said Dr. Francis. "Everything looks great. Want to hear the heartbeat?" She moved the wand inside Michelle again until a faint thumping came through the speakers.

"That's fast. One hundred and twenty beats per minute," I said.

"How did you know?" asked Dr. Francis.

"Chris is a musician," Michelle said, and she gripped my hand tight. I felt proud. Like I knew something about my child only I could know. Like this was what it was like to be a dad.

CON SORDINO
(with mute)
Michelle calls my inability to keep a secret "challenging." She's become an expert at spotting my divulgences before they happen. Whether it's at a party or we're out with friends, she senses when I'm about to drop a sensitive piece of information and intervenes with the skill of a professional handler. She can change the subject quicker than a politician. I've gotten better at keeping my mouth shut over the years, especially with Michelle's help. But I have to admit to a certain excitement that builds in me when I know something I want everyone else to know, a feeling that once I get the information out, the world will be a better

place. I was this way with the pregnancy. I discussed our baby names with mere acquaintances. I talked with fellow musicians about plans that were none of their business. I revelled in the constant congratulations and feeling that I had somehow joined an exclusive club. The daddy club. I was smoking the cigar before earning the right to be in the delivery room.

"You have to stop telling people," Michelle told me. "What if something goes wrong?"

"I haven't told *that* many people," I said.

"You told the guy who runs the bodega!" she said, and she was right, I had.

And I had. And I had.

LAGRIMOSO
(tearfully)
A week later, Michelle took the train during her lunch break to Dr. Francis's office. I was at home because we'd decided that I didn't need to be at every appointment; there were going to be a lot of them and this particular one was only a check-in.

"Call me as soon as you're done," I said.

She had to be back in her office at one o'clock. So at five minutes after one, I called her desk. I wanted to hear about what she'd seen on the monitor. I wanted to know how the little spud's arms were progressing. But Michelle wasn't there. I called every ten minutes for an hour. Finally, at two, she picked up. She'd been crying.

"Where have you been?" I asked. "Are you okay?"

"Something's wrong," she said. "The baby is smaller than it's supposed to be."

Smaller than it's supposed to be. Smaller than it's supposed to be. I ran the line over in my head trying to remember if I'd read anything in the hundreds of Google searches that I'd seen. "That doesn't sound too bad," I said. "Kids come in different sizes."

Michelle cried harder. "It should be eight weeks and it's only six," she told me. "The heartbeat is slower, too. It hasn't grown since our last appointment." She was trying to lower her voice, she didn't want everyone in her office to hear her crying. "I'm coming home," she said, and hung up.

Here's what we learned: in the early stages of pregnancy, the weekly size of your baby is very important. Dr. Francis told us there was a possibility we'd gotten the conception date wrong, that everything was still fine and that we'd know more in a week.

I dug into the Internet. I'd sneak out of bed in the middle of the night and spend hours online researching everything I could find on weekly gestation. The news was not good. Hundreds of mothers posting about the same problem. Gestation weeks that were off, posting in forums begging for help, any kind of information possible. And to be sure, there were a few miracles. Like the one from Mom_Zone234: "My baby wasn't growing and then all of a sudden, it sprung to life! Grew two weeks size in one week! Don't lose hope! Thank God. Thank God. It is a miracle!"

Michelle and I moved like we were under water that week. We stayed in, watched *Forrest Gump* three times, and two full seasons of *The Sopranos*. We ate Skinny Cow ice cream sandwiches and tried to forget what might be coming. I was angry at myself for having told people about the pregnancy too soon. Why had I said anything? I had jinxed it. I was the problem. Michelle meanwhile found extra hours somewhere in the day to push ahead on the thesis, her focus nothing short of miraculous.

"The fetus is still six weeks in size," Dr. Francis told Michelle and me as we sat in the examination room clinging to hope. She pushed the wand around inside Michelle until the heartbeat crept through the speakers.

"About eighty beats per minute," I said, and Dr. Francis nodded. "I've been reading about cases where the baby suddenly starts growing again," I said optimistically.

"I've been doing this for twenty years," Dr. Francis said. "I'm afraid the prognosis doesn't look good. I've never seen a pregnancy recover."

Michelle and I had talked during the week. If there were still a heartbeat we would wait, and Dr. Francis agreed. So we waited another week.

And another week. And another week.

After three more weeks, thirty beats per minute and the baby was still six weeks in size. Each week was a mix of hope and desperation. Our baby was dying before our eyes.

Dr. Francis had been telling us that Michelle would most likely miscarry, she was surprised it hadn't happened already. As the weeks pressed on and the heartbeat grew slower, the fear of the miscarriage followed Michelle everywhere she went.

"I don't want it to happen at work," she said to me one day when I met her for lunch. She hugged me and we cried together in the middle of Times Square. Red tour buses drove by, stacked with tourists taking pictures. There were throngs of people and neon signs. Michelle felt small in my arms in the biggest place in the world.

Dr. Francis was recommending a procedure called a D&C. We could check Michelle into the hospital in the morning and she'd be out that afternoon. "But there's still a heartbeat," I said. Michelle and I were back for yet another appointment. It was now twenty beats per minute. I could see the heartbeat on the monitor.

Take the slowest setting possible on a metronome (30 bpm).

Drop it by ten.

largheto: rather broadly (60–66 bpm).

largo: broadly (40–60 bpm).

lento: slowly (40–60 bpm).

grave: slow and solemn (20–40 bpm).

"Is this an abortion?" I asked Dr. Francis. She looked at me with sadness, the look of someone wanting to reassure me that what we were about to do would never be considered such a thing. "In my medical opinion this pregnancy must be terminated," she said. It sounded like she'd been practising the line since college.

"I want it to be over," Michelle said. She was sitting on the examination table, rolling the end of her paper robe between her fingers. Her head was down. She was crying. Dr. Francis took her hand, told her everything would be okay. I took one last look at the monitor before Dr. Francis shut it off. I could see the warble of the heartbeat, I could see the stubs of the baby's arms.

Michelle was in the recovery room still under anaesthetic. I'd been allowed in so I could be there when she woke up. She looked so tiny in that hospital bed. Worn out and fragile. Her short hair was sticking up in every direction and she looked pale. I had never seen my wife like this. I had never seen her so vulnerable. So beaten down. Her strength through this whole thing carved yet another space in my heart reserved only for her. *Always remember how much you love this woman,* I told myself.

"Is it gone?" she asked as her eyes blinked open. She looked around the room and for a second I didn't think she recognized me. "Baby, is it over?" she asked me again as she tried to focus.

"It's over," I said.

"Where am I?" she asked.

I told her she was in the recovery room, that everything had gone smoothly. "Can I have a glass of water?" she asked.

The attending nurse came over and helped her sit up, and I took the glass of water and put it to Michelle's lips. Her mouth was dry. Her lips were white, parched, and hard. Slowly she gained control of her hands, took the water under her own power, and had the nurse refill it. I sat there watching my wife, neither of us saying a word. Dr. Francis came in. "You did great," she said to Michelle. "I'm proud of you guys." I asked an awkward question about the baby, something about it looking alive. "It doesn't look like what you'd think," said Dr. Francis.

I felt a great sadness in that moment, for Michelle, for the situation we found ourselves in, for the decision we'd made to silence a heartbeat.

But there was something else, a kind of dread that came from the hopelessness of what we had in front of us. Getting pregnant again felt so far away. Could we go through it again? Not if this was the result.

No way. No way.

OBBLIGATO
(required, indispensable)

And there's that heartbeat. I still think about it today, nearly two years after our Chloe was born. I can feel twenty beats per minute in my body like it's a part of me, something I've taken on, a rhythm that guides me as I lift Chloe into a swing or help her down the slide. Like there's a life, as small and fleeting as it was, that gave up everything for this happiness. And what about the ethics of our decision? It's what stays with me now, long after. What are the ethics when there is no choice? So I have to ask myself, in those moments where the love for my daughter is so strong I think my heart can't take another second of it, *Where does life begin?* The best I can figure is that it starts in the heart, and grows from there.

CHRIS TARRY is a Canadian fiction writer and musician living in Brooklyn. His work has appeared or is upcoming in *The Literary Review*, *On Spec*, the *GW Review*, *PANK*, *Bull Men's Fiction*, and *Monkeybicycle*. In 2011 he was shortlisted for Ireland's Fish Short Story Prize and was a finalist in *Freefall* magazine's annual prose and poetry competition. Chris is also a four-time Juno Award winner and one of North America's most sought-after bassists. His most recent book, *Rest of the Story*, is a small collection of short fiction and a jazz album rolled into one.

Stork Bite

SADIQA DE MEIJER

1.

It's a home birth and then it isn't—meconium in the amniotic fluid; I don't see the spill, my belly is in the way, but I see the faces of my midwives cloud over. I'm in an ambulance without a siren. Flying down Johnson Street, recumbent, and the paramedics are cheerful—one is saying there should be more noise from me. Through the hospital, faces passing over me like streetlights, I don't care what they see. In a room, sips of coffee and pudding. Weak contractions. Oxytocin drip. Push and rest and push and rest. Partner and midwife and friend and nurse and doctor and resident and medical student and respiratory therapist. There are so many people in here, I say. The voices stop, except the friend who sings, the partner and nurse and midwife who say push. They see the hair. They see more hair. If I push harder I will rip myself apart and then I do and then the head is out. Pause. Last, easy push, then a purple, wailing baby upside down in someone's hands, whisked to a corner, suctioned and wrapped. She, they're saying, and congratulations, and she's heavy. Given to me. Give her to me, my born child arrived in the world of air, safely with me.

2.

My midwife shows me how to latch her. Says she looks wonderful, her breathing is a bit fast, but that can happen after a long labour, just ask the nurse to check later.

3.

Wide eyes, warm skin. Awe and accomplishment.

> *I have done what you wanted to do, Walt Whitman,*
> *Allen Ginsberg, I have done this thing,*
> *I and the other women this exceptional*
> *act with the exceptional heroic body.*†

Stars start to perforate the sky of the window. Beautiful first night. Alone together, partner home to clean for tomorrow — but he'll be back, we're splurging on a private room to sleep as three tonight.

Hello, hello, hello little being.

You're here you're here who are you.

Sleep.

4.

Four hours post-partum, we both wake up and she latches. When the nurse comes in, I tell her the breathing rate was high. She counts. Her wristwatch, my child's breath. Furrowed brow, another round of counting. She calls a second nurse. They call Neonatal Intensive Care. The resident reads the chart, stage-whispers *home birth* to the two people with him. Picks up my child.

Examine her here in my lap, I say.

He puts her down. Listens with his stethoscope, tells me she may have a heart defect. Keenly: his night just got interesting.

He takes her, places her in an incubator gurney. The team starts for the door. Are they really going to leave me here? My partner arrives right then, gets me into a wheelchair, and hurries us down the hall.

Neonatal Intensive Care Unit. We wash our hands at an enormous sink, put on yellow gowns. She's in a plastic case. They put a bracelet on her, monitor leads on her pink chest, oxygen prongs under her nose, tubes taped to her cheeks. They draw blood. She cries, but without tears. Her eyes are dark blue. We can touch her through holes in the sides of the incubator, so we sit on tall stools for hours, my hand on her skin. I don't want her to be away from me. It's too soon for that. But exhaustion sets in; I go to our room to sleep.

5.

We tag team, trying not to leave her alone. Nurses and monitors and alarms. I don't tell anyone that I went to medical school. I haven't practised medicine anyway, and I can't see how the information will help. I feel troublesome enough, having a midwife, wanting to breastfeed.

No matter what our midwife says to the doctors, I'm not allowed to breastfeed until our baby's respiratory rate slows to a certain number. To feed her, I have to leave the NICU, sit in a storage room and attach a suction cup to my nipples, pump out a dropperful of thick, cream-coloured colostrum that shudders through loops of plastic tubing into a container. I label it with my name and her name and birthdate, give it to the day's nurse, who puts it in a fridge, then warms it later, and injects it through a plastic tube that passes through our baby's nostril and esophagus into her marble-sized stomach. We're that far apart.

6.

Good news, says a different resident, there's meconium in the lungs but no signs of infection, you'll be home in two days. But that evening, the doctors change shifts. What I favour, says the new one, dark circles under her eyes, is a proactive approach. Two antibiotics, into the bloodstream. A seven- to ten-day course. She seems so well, we say, she's so alert and unfevered and with normal test results. But her blood oxygen, the reading from the clip on her foot, it's lower than it should be without the oxygen streaming into her nose. We watch the number drop whenever the tubes shift out of place. How to second-guess the doctor of the newborn and live with your consequences?

7.

The suspense in this account, it seems unfair; there's no need to draw it out.

Because the outcome is good.

For months afterwards, describing our time in the NICU to friends or acquaintances, I'm stumbling somewhere between thankfulness for how it ended and frustration with how it went.

Things happen and then the story forms in the tellings, never as complicated as the thing.

8.

Every shift, a new nurse, with no recurrences at first.

There is the blond woman in her forties who calls me mama, tells me about the stages to look forward to with our child, and while the specifics barely register, I'm grateful for her implicit message: a good future is waiting. She helps us bathe our daughter.

When I get to breastfeed again, three days after the birth, it's because a confident, possibly still teenage student nurse says, Try it, it's best for your baby. We try it, and the blood oxygen levels don't worsen. Hours later, it works again. And again. Morning comes and the doctors round, hovering over our crowded corner—incubator, monitors, IV pole, charts. This is the time to make my case, to say, No more tube in her stomach. But before I start, the new nurse, small in stature, puffs out beside me like a rooster and declares, This is a baby whose oxygen rises while nursing! She presents the records of oxygen saturation, and then I have permission to breastfeed.

9.

We're the marvelling new parents, taking in the scent, the expressions and fingernails and curled feet of our child. But the reveries are brief, interrupted by the medications, shift changes, alarms. When we hold her, we're afraid to dislodge the tiny IV and cause another round of pain. In my arms, plump and alert, she seems so indisputably fine. It's when we leave her that we are both visited by the terror that she'll get sicker.

It's not only a fear of her illness, which we don't have a name for. The fluid in her lungs may or may not clear on its own, she may or may not have pneumonia, and the question of a heart defect has been left unanswered. The admitting resident has told us her oxygen was low enough that there may be brain damage.

I'm also afraid of the NICU itself. My medical education allows me to envision the worst-case outcomes of every intervention. There is a hospital-borne infection present, potentially terrible. Two babies have it and we're told that ours is at risk, having been in the same resuscitation bed. The NICU is rearranged to create an isolation area. Each day, the doctors start rounding there and then cover the rest of the unit, and I eye their stethoscopes with suspicion, worried about contamination. It takes three days for our tests to come back negative. But each treatment has risks; the feeding tube can puncture her esophagus or stomach, the antibiotics can cause hearing loss and kidney damage, the IV site can get infected.

10.

After three nights, I am discharged as a patient. I'm healing well from a minor tear, all swellings going down. We meet with the NICU charge nurse. You don't live far away, she says, you can drive in at night to nurse. We don't have a car. She tells us to take a cab. I say that's not practical, twice a night, for me or for our baby. She says pump. I say it's not just the milk, I want to hold her. She tells me the latest studies say too much holding raises stress hormones in newborns. I say I'll put a sleeping bag in the visitor's lounge, I'm not leaving. A social worker is called. She performs some kind of bureaucratic miracle; we get a two-person room in a wing reserved for the families of ICU patients.

11.

Friends have arranged meal deliveries for us. Every day at the hospital doors, a basket or box or bag arrives. Real cutlery, plates—signals of homes. The weight of that food in my lap is the measure of care. I eat large meals, wanting to fill my child with the same nutrients and love.

12.

At eleven or so, we go to our room on another floor. Every three hours, a nurse calls me on the bedside phone—my baby's hungry—and I leap up, hurry down the corridor, always needing a bathroom stop to void what seems like litres of retained fluid, then the elevator, another dim corridor. I press the NICU buzzer and identify myself (_____'s mother, a phrase so unfamiliar and pleasing), scrub my hands, and walk among the aquarium incubators to take her, crying, from the arms of a night nurse. Often, I don't need the call—I sit up with a start, shirt soaked with milk. She's awake! And then the phone rings.

13.

Later, when I tell the story to our friends, I find I often talk about the nurses—but not the lovely ones. The others.

14.

Our baby is full term in a ward designed for premature babies; she's large for the incubator, and has the loudest cry. One nurse keeps muttering these dissatisfactions as she handles our daughter. Another, a few feet from us, complains that term babies just aren't cute.

I arrive to breastfeed late in the evening, and distorted guitars are blasting through our section of the NICU. The new nurse has a radio on beside the incubator, to keep herself awake. When she hands me my wailing daughter, she says, This isn't hunger, it's a temper tantrum—you'll have your hands full when this one's older. Our baby is five days old. Five days of gloved hands, needles, and drugs. Her incubator's heat has been raised to what a premature baby needs, not a term one—she's soaked in sweat. My partner goes and sits up at the incubator for the rest of the night.

Another nurse, addressing her student, says that our baby has a red mark on her neck because I'm holding her too much. I can't answer her; I'll cry and I refuse to do that. You know what, I say to the student, it's a birthmark, sometimes called a stork bite.

A new nurse tells my partner he's too large to be in the NICU at the same time as me.

On the next shift, I get parenting advice—again, it's a lesson against spoiling our baby through holding, and how will I do dishes or laundry if she gets too used to it—prefaced by "here in Canada."

They have our baby. They have her and we can't be there all the time—it's not permitted during shift changes, and impossible to sustain at every hour, even eating and sleeping and showering in shifts. Skilled and professional gestures can still be infused with anger; if we start fights, we leave her in those kinds of hands. So we stay selective about arguments, and focus on showing up.

15.

I start to struggle to show up. Poor sleep. Sutures and heavy ankles. Brief visits from anxious family, negotiations with nurses, shifting updates on risk and recovery. At the epicentre, her, newly separate—a small stranger who feels intimately familiar. Some of the usual means of getting to know each other are missing: I can't be alone with her, sleep or walk with her, put my own diapers or clothes or blankets on her. Instead of welcoming her to our space, I'm disoriented myself, and part of me wants to curl under bedcovers, sleep, read, eat sugary food, stop forcing myself across the threshold of the NICU, into what feels on certain shifts like hostile territory. My partner encourages me, back to the scrub sink, the armchair by the incubator.

Once I'm holding her again, I feel grounded. I whisper to her in my first language, tell her about the view: the lake and island, and if we turn, sometimes the ferry at the edge of its winter route. I used to have a small belief, when I was alone and walking, that when I looked down a side street and the ferry was there in the interval between buildings, that was good luck.

I try to leave only when she's asleep. The worst moments are when she wails and I still have to walk away, leave her in the incubator so that the nurses can change shifts or the doctors can make their rounds.

16.

Later, out in the world with my daughter, I sometimes daydream about running into one of the judgmental nurses, in a checkout line or parking lot, free to say what I think of them, their insistence that a newborn is safer in a plastic case than in her mother's arms.

17.

The work of the nurses is incredibly demanding. They are responsible for multiple newborns, some of whom don't breathe on their own. Alarms go off all the time, and virtually every time it's from a lead getting twisted or undone by a baby's movement—but the nurses can never tune them out, they have to distinguish each one from an actual emergency, perpetually ready to perform resuscitation. They implement all the orders for medication and treatments, take meticulous and constant notes, while also changing diapers, comforting, and bottle-feeding. They work in physically cramped, aesthetically bleak spaces, and their shifts are twelve hours long.

Parents who insist on being present all the time further increase the stress. We keep introducing minor chaos—we're awkward around equipment, react emotionally to medical decisions, and in our own case, make requests that create more work, such as calling us instead of using a soother. My partner and I thank each nurse for her care, but of course our actions are the louder statement, and put us at odds. We're supposed to offer our love and affection in doses, scheduled, appropriately, while my instinct is for a hugely inappropriate love, one that stays close sleeping and waking, holds her, sees her through.

18.

There are other families; as we get accustomed to the hospital routines, we notice them more. Parents who have had to make the NICU part of their days, weeks, and months, while returning to work, raising older children. Who are here for their second or third premature baby. Some call the nurses their angels.

The triplets, quietly heartbreaking—with a limit of two babies to an incubator, the tiniest lies alone, whimpering because he is too small to cry.

The baby who can't vocalize at all because there's a breathing tube separating his vocal cords. He needs a painful procedure; I'm present because I am breastfeeding beside him. The mouth of a wrinkled, minuscule human, releasing scream after scream, soundless.

The term babies with faintly yellow skin, coming in to lie under warm lamps, returning home in a day or two.

19.

I think I talk about the difficult nurses, afterwards, because the NICU was difficult, and so that subject strikes the right emotional pitch while protecting me and the listener from a conversation about the deeper difficulty. What it exempts me from saying is: that was the worst fear, what could have happened, nothing in life has mattered as much.

My partner and I rarely even talk about it between us. We've come up against danger and backed away, like the ferry bouncing back from those massive dark tires on the dock.

20.

Write a letter, say the friends—the hospital should know what happened to you. Months later I write a letter and then rewrite it and rewrite it and it sits on my computer going nowhere.

21.

We left the NICU after ten days.

We left with our well child.

There was other baggage for us to unpack over weeks and months and years. The same worries as most new parents, but closer to the surface. I was more cautious than the other mothers we knew. I made everyone who wanted to hold her wash their hands. I dressed our daughter in layers at the slightest breeze, checked on her breathing every night well into toddlerhood.

But the corollary of our dread came with us also—a profound appreciation of our baby's presence. That feeling carried me through a lot of sleeplessness. It allowed me to immerse myself in mothering without feeling too fraught over what wasn't getting done. If my pocket notebooks contained more scribbled letters to our daughter than notes toward new projects, that was my great luck.

22.

Luck. For a while, I felt a bright, eclipsing sense of that word, as if it illuminated me. I was home with a healthy child. I had seen just enough of the other babies, of binder charts thick with complications, to know that it could have been otherwise.

23.

Luck, undeserved and uncontrollable. But I don't operate as if that's true.

I remember trying not to turn my back on my daughter in the incubator, shuffling away backwards because turning around felt wrong.

The lake ice broke during those ten days. Every morning, more glitter and motion in the view; that seemed like a good sign.

With friends, part of the reason I wasn't talking about what could have happened was that I still feared invoking it.

I wasn't sending my letter of complaint, because even appropriate concerns seemed to betray the luck of having access to a NICU, and of leaving with each of us intact.

24.

In the story I read to my daughter this morning, a father catches a clump of weeds in his fishing net, then an old sandal. He decides to have lunch; maybe his luck will change. His child wants to use the net. Sure, says the father — I'm not having any luck anyway.

An interval or break, meant to make luck turn. Luck, good or bad, clinging to a person for a day or a year or a lifetime.

25.

The word superstition sounds so dismissive.

"A belief or practice," says my dictionary, "resulting from ignorance, fear of the unknown, trust in magic or chance, or a false conception of causation."

A word in the vocabulary of those oriented to rationality and not strangeness.

But science is strange, too: everything that happened outside in daylight, projectable somewhere on a massive screen the size of space, because of the constant speed of light.

The weary doctor telling us that there's little evidence of an infection, but she'll sleep better if the antibiotics are started — and us saying okay, not asking where between the rational and superstitious that decision falls.

Or the friends bringing us meals. At moments, those parcels seemed a bit like offerings to me. Not that I made assumptions about intent, but I felt there was an undercurrent of thanks in their daily arrival, our family as lightning rod. Which, in an unsuperstitious sense, we were — reducing for a time the odds that any of our friends would encounter the NICU.

26.

During our NICU stay, people prayed for us in Arabic and English and Dutch. It mattered, of course. It was comforting and moving.

But what I'm getting at now isn't as formal as prayer. It's the improvised, unspoken practices that exist outside of what religions or cultures make repeatable and communal. Probably we all have them, whatever else we believe. In each of us, a kind of accumulated structure, a scaffold of rituals and omissions, based on the patterns we discern from our experiences. Small or elaborate, used hourly or only in crisis. And mostly we can't say how much it works or doesn't work—it operates so privately. Something curious and halfway functional, built of twigs and tissue paper.

27.

I saw Marjorie Beaucage's film *BINGO!*‡ this year. An exploration of her own luck structure, glimpses of those of others. It could be a form of portraiture, eccentric and precise, a representation more intimate than how we appear.

28.

My perspective is slanted through the lens of a good outcome. I can't predict what would have happened otherwise—possibly my structure would have burned to ash, before I even surmised its contours.

29.

So this is what I have: what happened.

The thing, more complicated than any telling. The inkling that it brought, almost a latent side effect, of the frame I've built for luck. There it stands, part of a wider strangeness that I try to dwell in often, writing or drawing. Ferries, waves, islands. One day, with luck, I'll need to explain to my daughter what I chose. Not medicine, not that clearly helpful work, but an odd accumulation of sketches and words.

Maybe I will show her the poem that, years before anything, I tore from a Dutch newspaper, carried with me until it was an illegible rag:

Poëzie

Zoals je tegen een ziek dochtertje zegt:
mijn miniatuurmensje, mijn zelfgemaakt
verdrietje, en het helpt niet;
zoals je een hand op haar witte voorhoofd legt,
zo dun als sneeuw gaat liggen,
en het helpt niet:
zo helpt poezie.

— Herman de Coninck§

Poetry

The way you say to a sick little daughter:
my miniature human, my tiny homemade
sorrow, and it doesn't help;
the way you lay a hand on her hot forehead,
as thinly as snow lies down,
and it doesn't help:
so poetry helps.

(translated with permission, for the purpose of
this essay only)

SADIQA DE MEIJER's writing has appeared in various literary journals and been included in *The Best Canadian Poetry in English 2008* and in the anthology *Villanelles*. Her poetry won the 2012 CBC Poetry Prize. Her first book of poems is *Leaving Howe Island* (Oolichan, 2013).

NOTES
†Sharon Olds, "The Language of the Brag," *Satan Says* (Pittsburgh: University of Pittsburgh Press, 1980), 44–45.
‡*BINGO!*, directed by Marjorie Beaucage, 1991. Video (Black & White, Stereo, 17:47).
§Herman de Coninck, "Poezie," *Met een Klank van Hobo* (Amsterdam: Van Oorschot, 1980).

The Red River

ERIKA CONNOR

I HAD A MISCARRIAGE in Mali, West Africa, on March 21, 2003. I was thirty-eight. Three days later I flew home to Canada. I told my family, but I kept my feelings to myself. There was nothing to refer to, no ceremony, no wisdom, no resolution for what had taken place. I came back from a journey to the underworld.

It was the hot season in Bamako, in a suburb on the banks of the Niger. We were lying on a mattress on the earth in the tiny courtyard of our apartment, as if we were the only ones in the world. We were in some kind of trance. Issa was lying with his face on my belly. I was pregnant, radiating with life, all my senses were strong. I had a vision of that little lamp-lit village on the plains where we had ridden in on the sand tracks two months ago, under a black star-lit sky, on a cart pulled by two black bulls. That was when conception had happened, I knew.

Issa had heard about terracotta masks hidden there in a tomb and he had gone to ask permission to dig. The chief and villagers didn't seem to mind as long as we paid and made our offerings. It was a tomb from an old war with their enemies, but I thought it is never a good thing to dig in a tomb.

The *koromogho*, or diviner, lived in the hut next door and we went to see him. He gathered a handful of sand and poured it into our hands and we whispered and blew gently on it and sifted it back into the man's hands. He spread it out on the floor, looking for ripples and marks, and lay his fingerprints in patterned rows that looked like two-headed figures. He kept seeing the twins.

That night the wind blew through the trees, blew the dust up into the air and the clouds travelled fast across the full moon. The earth glowed as cattle slept nestled in their straw. In our clay room lit by one hurricane lamp we were filled with desire. The wind blew all around us, bowing the metal roof. Issa had found something in the tomb, a fragment of clay, part of an ancient face. This is what we carried back.

"How can we keep it?" I asked incredulous. "You have no money, no security, no passport, no papers, no visa. We come from different countries, different cultures, we speak different languages."

We had been through this over and over again for years. A wave of panic came over me. It brought back my abortion from a time before Issa. I couldn't do it again. I was filled with horror and unbearable tenderness.

I couldn't sleep. Issa took me walking the back streets at midnight. There was an owl on a telephone wire. Small and pale, it turned its dark eye on us. Issa made a cry and it flew off, white-winged over the rusty corrugated rooftops and palms.

"It's a messenger," I said.

"Of what?"

"I don't know."

Of death, of course. We didn't know the little thing inside of me was going to let go.

For four years, over the waves of the Atlantic, I made the long journey to be with Issa, from the boreal forests of western Quebec to the dust and thorn trees of the Sahel, shoreline of the Sahara. From the blue river that ran cold and quick through the northern pines to the red river that snaked up through the sands to Timbuctu and beyond.

My love of West Africa began long before Issa. I rode by bush taxi, donkey cart, pirogues, anything to take me into the heart of the old places. I had my sketchbooks and journals to capture how it felt. Ever since I was a child I have expressed myself through paint, clay, and words.

Once I rode a white horse into Kayes, on the border of Senegal and Mali, and met Issa. He was working at the inn where I stayed. I was drawn to him and the land that had formed him, the baking clay, blowing dust, turbulence and tenderness, the laughter despite the thorns. Eldest son of an antique dealer, with a large family to support up north, he went haunting the hotels, the market alleys, listening for the word, picking up trails: tourists to guide, cars to sell, trucks to transport. He looked at me with my white horse. Maybe he thought I was an omen. Maybe I reminded him of the local saying: "When a white horse arrives in the village, good fortune will come."

The air in Issa's dark back room hung still and hot. Voices came from the street, as if I lay far away at the bottom of a well. Children brushed their hands across the metal door. The burning light from the earth seeped into the air vents like stars.

Small drops of blood appeared at noon and the pain came swiftly. There was a knife inside me that dug a little deeper each time. Every singing fibre rippled up the razor's edge and there was no end to this song. I struggled out to the outhouse and found Aisha, the neighbour's girl, lazing on the floor in the front room where there was no furniture. She had come in through the open door as usual. She said nothing, just looked up at me with her large dark eyes, quiet, haunting, as if she knew. A guardian angel.

I could hear her softly singing. There was too much blood. It came in clumps and disappeared into the dark hole of earth. There was too much pain. What was I supposed to do? Where was Issa? I imagined going out into the street with the sand in my sandals, across cigarette butts, goat pellets, children's footprints, along the cracks in the clay walls, the smell of urine stains. Who would I ask? Was it an omen, a curse? Was there a ceremony? I felt like I was meant to untangle the strands of broken fibre so that I could begin again to weave the world, but I didn't know how.

Aisha was gone. Night had fallen. I woke up to a shadow at the door. Issa. Not a word, just his face staring. I heard my voice.

"Take me to the hospital."

༄ I was lying in the back of a yellow taxi, looking up at the moving globes of street lamps, moons, stars, and the line of the wires, everything strung together. I worried about the stains of blood. I worried about losing my mind. How had it happened? But the windows were all open, or maybe they could never be closed. There was no glass. I was floating in the hot wind, among the voices of night people, singing, sirens, smells of sewer, diesel and sizzling coals, the beeps of nightjars and bats. Palm fronds swept over street lamps, candles flickered on clay. Now we were crossing the bridge, going to the only hospital, the one Issa's friends joked about, calling it "la morgue." I could smell the cool waters that run through the Sahara, lifeblood, what they called "Joliba," the red river. The ritual calabashes were floating. The blood pooled warm between my legs. I could smell the sea. The same. We come from the same.

༄ Long ago, in the first year, Issa and I had waded into the river reeds, each with a calabash of fresh milk balanced on our palms and seven floating kola nuts divided between us. I had three and he had four. He was dressed in traditional white lace tunic and pants. I wore a linen camisole and a pale wrap of beige and pink geometric patterns.

It was Issa's idea to offer prayers for our protection, to help us in our struggle to be together. The kola nut is sacred to the ancestors. It is also given to the bride's mother in the traditional marriage ceremony.

I was silent, feeling the water on my thighs, watching Issa, then, like him, I tossed the calabash over my shoulder and did not look back. This was the *ʃedaka*, a blessing for water and all that it gives.

I had a dream I was floating in the Gatineau River when I sank like a stone. It amazed me that I had forgotten how to swim. I was just a weight and so I let go. But, by some miracle, I was tied to a rope that was also tied to Issa and he just pulled me up again. Strange, since he had never learned to swim.

֍ Issa walked ahead across the hospital grounds. Why did he leave me behind? Like I was an old woman or a small child, learning to walk again, hobbling past the bougainvillea and crickets, the humid, tangling mass of it, toward a light on an open patio. A night intern was having a cigarette and a cat went slinking past, its movement like silk, as if we were close to the sea. I could hear the thundering inside me.

Issa came back for me, a sombre stillness in his face, his eyes looking down. This was the way here. All thoughts and actions held energy. Sickness must not be enticed. This was a woman's mystery and men were afraid. I knew that deeply, but still I ached for comfort, for some reassurance, some kindness.

He led me down the lit hall open to the night, to a small room off the side where five women nurses were busy eating and laughing, fried yams and hot sauce staining a piece of brown paper on the desk. Issa went out into the hallway. The large woman behind the desk motioned me to a wooden bench behind her. This was where I lay while the women's voices carried me through the waves, their warbling and clucking like the chickens of my barnyard youth. Each wave was a monumental journey and the noisier they were the better, so they would not hear my pain.

֍ I kept the little photo slip from the ultrasound, the floating waves in the darkness, ghostlike. A little outline, like a drawing on a cave wall, a little spirit barely there, of what was once there, head, spine, on the right side of my womb facing left.

I remember the little dark room cluttered with cabinets, brown bottles, tools lying on counters, garbage on the floor, and the old ultrasound machine, and how the technician was unfriendly, slopping the cream on my stomach. I remember his words when he held out the photo and pointed it out, how one part was there, the other over there. It had broken up, fragmented. Issa would not come near, turned his face away. But it drew me as to a window. This had happened in my body. I had done this, saying we couldn't keep it. I carried a dead body and would have to have it flushed out. The blue scrawl of the man's pen made waves of energy.

(119 x 62 57 mm) On note une masse hétérogène au niveau
du fond, pouvait évoquer une grossesse arrêtée, au total.

In many dreams I tried to give birth, but the being had turned to stone and that was why I was sick. My stomach was swollen and there was a tumour growing to the right side like a second navel. There was something wrong with me, but I tried to hide it.

A man in a white coat led me to another room that looked like a storage room for metal beds. He motioned for me to lie down on a board that had been laid across the springs. He pulled away all the layers of cloth and cotton wadding and it was like a dam that had given way. He jerked his hand away.

"Mon Dieu, le sang. C'est trop!"

He stuffed all the cloths quickly back again and left me there. I thought of the women in the desert and how their vaginas were sewn together with silk thread and acacia needles, gum and sugar, ash and goat dung to cauterize and how their husbands used a razor blade or knife to reopen it.

I lay on the hard bed in the room of blue chipped paint and smell of Mercurochrome and sweat. Was this how I was going to die? A paradox: that in creating life by accident I was now being led into death. The Egyptian word *mes* meant "to give birth," and the hieroglyph depicted the skins of three dogs. Guardians of the underworld.

The red river is a place I know well, of sand banks and gardens, egrets and drinking cattle, sparseness and sustenance. But it is deeper also, the blood that every woman knows. It is the first taboo of the world, first sacrifice, first offering. It is the red of the priestess's robes. Water is the blood of the earth.

They led me to another room. The young man was soft and smiling, saying he had to check the position of my uterus. With a gloved hand between my legs and the other hand on my belly, he went up the broken, twisted channels, my tormented wounds, and I fought intrusion.

"Mais, il faut se calmer."

A woman came in with a flowered headscarf and went to sit behind the desk. She asked me to call in my friend. I sat with difficulty; the blood had already soaked through my pants. Issa sat beside me, uncomfortable, watching as I counted the money. She took my money and counted it again. The payment came before the service like any ceremony. She explained the procedure. The womb had to be cleaned out. They would put me to sleep. She would perform the operation. Her face was kind and strong, light-skinned. She said she was from Morocco. I thought of the Berbers in the High Atlas, ancestors of the Immazigh, who some thought were the Amazons. There was something numinous about her. She was going to free death from my womb. I gave her my blessing.

They wheeled me over the stained cement floor into a large echoing room and placed me on the stretcher with my feet in the braces. I saw the tray: strange instruments, needles, knives, and coloured liquids. The fluorescent lights were flickering above, crickets sang through the open window slats, a line of tiny ants was moving down the wall. The Moroccan woman and two young men were arranging things, talking softly in their language.

A man laid a sheet over me, saying, "Tout va bien."

I thought of my family. No one knew I was here. My heart was pounding. There was nothing I could do. They tapped the IV into my arm and I felt the bitter liquid in my mouth. And then I was gone.

I was coming back from a very long journey, along an old pathway. I imagined a forest. So many forks in the road, configurations inside of me, corridors, networks. I was trying to remember the way. Where was I and where did I have to go? Someone was walking alongside me and I was singing, telling him what I was seeing, talking my way back to the world. I saw that it was Issa, following the stretcher back to the room. He helped to lift me onto the bed. I began to cry.

"We couldn't help it. He didn't want to be born."

Issa laid his hand on my face to stop the tears. I met eyes with the young woman lying in the next bed.

"She carried her baby for eight months and lost it to malaria."

I looked into her eyes and saw how it was. This was the mystery of women, despite politics, economy, despite what you ate or how you prayed. Despite my abortion years ago, despite the fact that Issa lived here and I lived there and there were no immigration papers, not enough money, no apparent solution. I had lost flesh and blood on this earth where I had not been born.

The night went on. Over the wall partitions I could hear voices, the *shush, shush* of sandals making their way down the hall, the crickets. Issa slept on my bed, in respect, with his feet at my head, his head at my feet. He held my bare feet warm in his hands. It would never leave me. I had been given life.

The souls of the unborn children are still with me. I made a clay sculpture of a baby boy smiling, holding a snake around his neck. At his feet lies a dog. On his left is an owl in a tree. Behind him is a swimming fish. One day maybe I will return to the red river and perform my own ritual burial.

What about the dreams I had of the boy and the girl? What about the vow of childlessness I made at sixteen, standing in front of my parents, traumatized by their divorce? What of the words I told Issa coming out of anaesthesia that he would not remember and that I did not write down? Like him I never spoke about it, never asked myself how I felt, until I called him once, years later, on the day of the anniversary.

I read that the placenta must be retrieved after death to ensure the soul's release. Was there one? What did they do with the remains at the hospital? Did they ask me? I don't remember. It happened in Africa, ancient place of ritual.

I dreamed that I was rolling a large lump of earth through the forest. Inside the ball of earth was a seed. Along the way a tree caught it with its branches and began to strike it down into the ground, burying it. It has sowed the seed for me.

ERIKA CONNOR is an artist, writer, and art teacher from rural Quebec, with a BFA in studio art and creative writing from Concordia University in Montreal. She won the Irving Layton Award for Best Fiction in 1991. She is published in the US anthologies *Travelers' Tales: The Best Travel Writing* (2008, 2009, 2011, 2012) and *The Best Women's Travel Writing* (2006, 2010). She is currently sending out her writing, and working on novels and non-fiction. She has travelled by horse in Senegal, Mali, and Mongolia, and volunteered at the wild Przewalski horse reserve in Mongolia, at a dog shelter in India, on an agricultural program in Togo, and in Ottawa for a wild bird rehabilitation centre and the Humane Society's Brightening Lives program. She lives in a cabin in the Outaouais and is interested in traditional arts and survival skills, and living close to nature.

Missing Data

LAURA ROCK

WHEN I LOST A pregnancy for the first and only time, there was no Internet, not really. Maybe there was the beginning of the Internet. In 1994, e-mail still seemed like a miracle of efficiency. Researching symptoms online meant going to the websites of early content providers like Yahoo, clicking the Health category, and waiting a long time for the page to load. Another option: searching government or medical organization websites. This required a certain amount of knowledge about the embryonic web, soon to surprise us with its all-consuming demands.

My miscarriage—a generic term, inaccurate when it comes to me and my loss—was pre-Google and pre-social media. Today, typing "partial molar pregnancy" into Google's search engine yields 141,000 results in 0.13 seconds. Filtering data, not finding it, has become the important task.

Internet resources, unlike old-school books, come swaddled in virtual social support. We live in the age of e-nurturing. Health advice websites are staffed with nurses answering questions in real time, although the answers seem scripted enough to be generated by software. On one site, a chat dialogue box opened and "Tracy" introduced herself. I typed: "Can an embryo in a partial molar pregnancy ever develop fully?" Tracy, a paragon of reflective listening, responded, "You want to know about partial molar pregnancy. Is that right?" I clicked Yes and after a few moments, she sent me a link to the American Pregnancy Association website. Online forums allow sufferers and survivors to exchange insights in long, threaded conversations posted for public edification. You can update your Facebook status with a miscarriage announcement and immediately receive condolences, sad-face emoticons, and prayers. You can blog about it; faithful readers will comment. A Twitter user known as @caffeinated_mom recently live-tweeted her son's birth, noting slyly that the newborn wasn't her first Twitter baby. No doubt miscarriages in progress have been documented similarly.

Now you might think, What does it matter? A woman was expecting a baby for a few weeks, and then she wasn't. That fact is unassailable, that experience as old as motherhood. But the technology of the day makes a difference, not only in the medical outcomes of pregnancy — clearly it does — but also in shaping our understanding of the physical process, which in turn shapes how we feel.

Even without instant updates and virtual sharing, I saw myself back then as a proactive decision maker, giving informed consent, taking control. Now I realize that data have limits; the body follows its course whether or not the monitors are turned on. I've consented first and understood later, sometimes much later. And control is a joke — anyone with children will testify to that. Experience, learning, becoming tougher: the years after a loss change its meaning. Memories shift, rearranging themselves into a new order. I'm taking a backward look at that summer almost twenty years ago when I lost a life that I was carrying, the life that would have entered the world as my second child.

First baby first, though, because the fact of already having a child alters the experience of miscarriage. Also, the first delivery, in retrospect, has been recast in my mind as a series of misunderstandings. While it was a success according to the ultimate criterion — a healthy baby delivered — if it were a film I'd call it *Epic Information Fail*. Or maybe *Birth Bloopers*. A pattern was being established.

For a woman in her first pregnancy, every new sensation is a marvel, even heartburn and aching, vein-riddled legs. Even puking for the cause. I remember vividly the first time I felt the baby move. We were then living in the beltway suburbs of Maryland surrounding Washington, DC, where I worked for a government agency involved in international trade. I was on a business trip to Ottawa, taking part in the NAFTA negotiations.

There I sat in a bland, overheated boardroom with US, Canadian, and Mexican trade officials (mostly men, all older) seated around the conference table, wearing a grey pinstriped maternity suit that I recall as fashionable in cut and fabric, though certainly not fabulous by today's maternity-wear standards. Without warning, a tiny flutter tickled my lower abdomen. A subtle movement, but purposeful. I gasped and sat back carefully as the talk flowed around me. That this happened during a discussion of the NAFTA rules of origin—technical provisions underpinning free trade agreements—seemed hilarious, even though those rules had nothing to do with the origin of life. Still: origin, funny. Do it again, I thought, hand on belly, and my daughter responded by performing a little backflip, or so it seemed. And I controlled my face and kept this interior knowledge secret, because it would have been unprofessional to speak of it. The game then, for so-called career women (that odious term), was to pretend nothing was happening during pregnancy, and once the children arrived, not to talk about them at work. It wasn't smart; it wasn't done unless you wanted to be mommy-tracked (even more odious). That's something else that has changed for the better in the last two decades. Young women and men share their parental pride and family-related needs in the workplace far more openly. Sometimes I'm jealous that they have so much latitude.

What to Expect When You're Expecting was in its second edition when I, at the age of twenty-eight, found myself on the verge of new motherhood. (Strangely, it took about a year after my baby's birth before I could refer to myself as a mom without air quotes, the same time lag after the wedding before I could say the word "wife" without bursting out laughing. Change is difficult.) I read every page of *What to Expect*, even the last chapters, which laid out a sobering variety of potential problems. I began to frequent the women's health section of the bookstore; the stack of self-help manuals on our coffee table grew.

I felt fortunate to be able to consult these resources, and more advanced than previous generations. Just as I didn't have the Internet answers or Twitter feeds that today's pregnant women take for granted, my mother and mother-in-law didn't even have good books, and women's magazines were coded for a more delicate sensibility and therefore useless. My mother was knocked out for her three deliveries in the sixties, has no memory of them, and she was encouraged not to breastfeed, so she didn't. Of course my father wasn't present at my birth; men paced the waiting room and smoked. (I feel sorry for those men, kept offstage for the important scenes.) So it was with amusement that I observed my father-in-law flipping through *What to Expect* as he sat in our living room one day. He reminded me of a tourist visiting an exotic locale. I wondered what he would make of the graphic descriptions—so much female physicality, so little prettified: childbirth, with diagrams! He and his wife raised five children; it wasn't that he was uninitiated, but perhaps willfully ignorant of certain details. A family anecdote has it that he dropped off my mother-in-law at the hospital to have their fourth child and then went home to watch the rest of the hockey game.

His reaction to the reading material? Silent fascination until he reached the problem chapters and then he laughed nervously and muttered, "Gee, a lot can go wrong, can't it?" before setting the book down. His uncharacteristic commentary (he was typically a quiet participant in family life), his embarrassment mixed with engrossment—these have stuck in my memory as a reaction to too much information.

Information conveys power, though. In the early nineties, a shakeup of childbirth practices was under way. Hospitals in our area were then beginning to convert their sterile delivery rooms into birthing suites.

The notion that a rocking chair and teddy bear wallpaper could comfort a woman surfing the violent waves of labour seemed ludicrous, but at least it was a gesture toward privacy, and recognition of birth as a sacred family event rather than an illness to be cured.

Myriad facts were foisted on Tim and me at the childbirth classes we attended with other couples. The fathers were coached in being helpful yet not intrusive, ever ready to slide ice chips between parched lips or massage lower backs with tennis balls. The mothers were taught how to breathe through contractions — hee hee haw, hee hee haw. This doesn't work, but it can distract.

My girlfriends were having babies too, and so were several colleagues, albeit surreptitiously, until the belly became undeniable in the office. Most of us were inclined to explore natural childbirth but unsure that we'd be able to go through with it. My militantly anti-doctor friend was sure, though: she followed the Bradley school of thought, which held that medical interventions impeded the body in its primordial task. For example, during labour the cervix dilates and effaces, becoming softer in a process that my friend, citing the Bradley book, likened to a turtleneck stretching to allow your head through (an image I haven't been able to forget, unfortunately). To prepare for birth, she had her husband massage her perineum nightly, tugging at the vaginal opening to increase its elasticity. Hearing this, I felt a sudden rush of sympathy for my father-in-law and everyone like him.

The point is, we mothers of the nineties discovered options and the will to exercise them. Women were encouraged to draw up birthing plans and communicate them to doctors in advance, so that their "preferences" (easily forgotten in the heaving and sweating of labour) would be honoured. The birthing plan was a quasi-legalistic approach, but I appreciated its underlying motivation of empowering women to take back childbirth from the medical establishment.

Yet I couldn't help feeling, now and again, that this obsession with choice amounted to so much rich-world myopia. Shortly after the fall of the Communist government in Albania, I came across an article about Albanian women labouring in maternity wards two or three to a bed. A baby boom was straining the hospitals. Maternal mortality remains astonishingly high in many countries; childbirth is still a dangerous event for millions of women. Compare, for example, Chad's 2010 maternal mortality ratio of 1,100 per 100,000 live births with the Canadian, US, and Mexican numbers, respectively: 12, 21, and 50 according to UN Millennium Development Goals Indicators.

And here's the paradox: all the information we were pouring into our birthing plans was still incomplete, based on theoretical labour, ideal delivery. Key facts were missing. Until it happens, no one knows how an actual labour will go—what a person's real pain threshold is, whether the baby will thrive or not, if contractions will progress quickly or stall for days. We were about to find out.

Child number one, our Molly, arrived on schedule at Holy Cross Hospital, a huge facility in Silver Spring, Maryland, known locally as a baby factory. My OB/GYN was a fiftyish woman, small in stature, grey-streaked hair held in a bun. I liked her calm, no-nonsense demeanour, which undoubtedly derived from her experience delivering thousands of babies. I intensely disliked her office staff, however—every visit netted a hassle or bad attitude. They brimmed with indifference.

Since I was less assertive than I pretended to be while reading self-help books, in the end my birthing plan consisted of a few preferred scenarios I suggested to the doctor: natural childbirth if possible—here I waffled, conceding that my wimpy self might not be up to a drug-free delivery—and no episiotomy. I had read that this procedure—small cuts around the vagina to relieve pressure during delivery and stitched up afterward—was unnecessary, didn't work, and caused discomfort and scarring that lingered for months. She was skeptical: "No episiotomy, even if there's a risk of tearing?" No, not even then.

My water broke on my due date, in a restaurant. I may have left for the hospital too early—a first-timer, everyone was treating me like an unexploded bomb—but the nurses confirmed that I was in labour and kept me there. They urged me to walk the hallways to speed up the contractions. At no point in your life do you feel less like going for a walk, but Tim and I dutifully shuffled down the corridor and back again. After just a few hours, my contractions, though killing me, were barely discernible to the doctor. She declared that labour wasn't progressing as quickly as it should and decided to juice it with oxytocin. I said yes: who wants to prolong labour?

Then I agreed to anaesthesia to deaden the pain. My rational inner analyst knew that an epidural can slow down labour, but the prospect of numbness was too enticing. The anaesthetist made me bend over for a shot in the spine, warning that I could be paralyzed if I moved suddenly—like a contraction? I thought, panicking—but it was soon completed. Events had been set in motion, leading to an amicable divorce between my preferences and me.

Labour took off after that. All in, it lasted only six hours. Shortly after 1:00 AM, Molly emerged, eight pounds and six ounces of glory. The nurses set her on my chest for a few wondrous moments before whisking her away. Tim and I couldn't stop looking at her over in the warming pan, crying and kicking her legs.

Then the afterbirth was delivered—a bit of discomfort, but who cares, we had our baby—and then, not long after, I began to hemorrhage. A nurse checking on my blood flow discovered it and urgently called the doctor back. Luckily, she had not left the hospital.

When you are bleeding uncontrollably, when your mother hears the word "hemorrhage" and faints in the hallway, when doctors come running and begin "massaging" your uterus (that sounds soothing, doesn't it?) and you begin a round of screaming, and your normally reserved Canadian husband yells at the Americans to stop hurting you, and your blood pressure drops to the point that spots appear before your eyes and you start to black out, and you are transfused with two units of blood, and finally a decision is made to pack your uterus with gauze to stop the bleeding—in that moment, you don't worry about the birthing plan. And immediately afterward, when colour returns to your cheeks, and you look around at all the serious medical people doing what they're trained to do, you don't wish you were in a gussied-up birthing suite listening to Bach. You pray, thank God the child is fine, whatever else happens.

A few days later, I left the hospital with our baby, a stranger's blood in my veins, and a few stitches down there—the remnants of my unwanted episiotomy. Later still, in the doctor's office for the one-week checkup, I demanded facts. Why did I hemorrhage, what caused it, were there warning signs that could have predicted it? The doctor looked thoughtful and said, "Well, she *was* a big baby, and it *was* a fast labour. Sometimes it happens." And I thought, Yes, labour went quickly because you augmented it. She had been impatient; I blamed her for it. In fairness to her, however, I would not have chosen a thirty-six-hour labour. Everyone's heard stories of endless pain, babies in distress, emergency C-sections. No one can see the future.

The doctor's snippy assistants were suddenly interested in me. They couldn't stop talking about my drama. The receptionist, the one I couldn't stand, said, "They were going to have to do a hysterectomy if the gauze didn't work. Did you know that? It was a very close call."

To think of undergoing a hysterectomy at twenty-eight—hysterical, short daisy-chain to hysteria. This was a nugget of data I didn't know was missing, hadn't thought to ask about, wasn't told. A fact that didn't happen.

A year after Molly was born, I became pregnant for the second time. It was exciting to anticipate another baby, new joy on the way. The only worry, still far off, was the delivery: would I hemorrhage again? It is human nature to fixate on the last thing to go wrong, but that thing might be random.

I was exhausted, still adjusting to being a working mother (why do we have all these categories?). It was premature to disclose the pregnancy, much too soon for those how-my-absence-will-be-managed conversations. I waited until the twelve-week milestone.

In July we announced our news, on a visit to my mother's house. We had a picnic. I rolled around in the sweet-smelling grass with Molly, basking in sunshine; our little genius entertained the relatives with precocious babble while Tim and I swelled with pride. Then, within a day of telling, the spotting began: not much blood, sporadic and dark. I frantically searched the back pages of *What to Expect* and found nothing good. This could be a miscarriage or harmless, but either way the advice was go to bed and see the doctor as soon as possible. We were a six-hour drive from home. It was a sombre return trip.

The next day, the doctor squirted cold goop on my belly and made multiple passes through it with the probe, pushing into my skin until it hurt, searching for a fetal heartbeat, not finding one. She listened for a long time before I was sent to get an ultrasound.

I attended both appointments alone, clueless. But that's what happens with subsequent children. In a first pregnancy, your partner ideally is present for all the stages. Later, you're both too busy making a living or caring for other children. I went alone, feeling more competent than I was.

The ultrasound technician kept her face turned away from me, her shoulders hunched. She said nothing throughout the procedure, and that was troubling. When the baby is developing on schedule, the technicians almost always provide a play-by-play as they carry out their investigations, freeze-framing and measuring, collecting vital data. After that they might turn the screen around to let the mother have a look at the fuzzy shadows that represent the baby, maybe even pointing out some anatomy. But this ultrasound was different. When I gathered the courage to ask if everything was okay, she said, "Your doctor will get the report." It was a definitive answer, but not to the question I had asked. No shit, I wanted to say. Thanks for nothing.

My sorrow and fear took the form of rage: what about my rights, my right to be informed? I was an adult, capable of understanding what the test results revealed. But no—the doctor had to be the one to interpret: that was protocol.

I went home and phoned the doctor's office. It was the receptionist— now kind enough to ignore protocol, adversity turning her into an ally I didn't want—who confirmed that the pregnancy was over. Probably I had another consultation with the doctor, but I don't remember that. Somehow I was made to understand that I had to have a dilation and curettage, or D&C, at the hospital under anaesthesia. No other options were presented. The procedure was arranged.

That afternoon, at home, I called my friend and neighbour, the mother of a playmate of my daughter's. I felt the need to report to someone, and Tim, working at a construction site, was impossible to reach. This woman is the only person I know who never code-shifts: no matter who she's talking to, she says what she thinks. What she thought was that I should come over right this instant, and what the fuck was I doing sitting at home alone? Trying to be a frigging martyr?

I was just informing her. I didn't need anything.

"Get your ass over here," she said.

I hadn't thought I was traumatized in any way, but sitting in her cozy sunken living room with its picture window facing a hillside perennial garden, a wall of brilliant flowers rising before us, cradling a mug of hot tea, I allowed her to bathe me in sympathy and conversation, allowed myself to weigh the trauma, to huddle with it for a peaceful span of time before composing myself again. Female companionship was a gift that day.

And then the rationalizing began. I didn't feel entitled to be upset by the miscarriage. How *could* I be upset? We already had a child, I thought. We've conceived before and we'll do it again. Count blessings. These things happen. It's just nature, nature's code. My brain spewed clichés in the attempt to stave off feeling. Thinking was paramount, analysis necessary to pinpoint the cause. I was not alone in trying to figure out what had gone wrong, because everyone, well intentioned or not, had to opine. Too much stress, not enough vitamins or not the right ones (never mind that I was taking the alphabet), overwork, under-sleep, God's plan, my fault. Miscarry: like carrying the ball forward and fumbling it. Like mistake. Like miscarriage of justice. These thoughts linked hands and noisily marched in circles behind my eyes, inside my ears, deep within my rib cage, at night in my dreams.

The D&C was an outpatient procedure. I sank under the lull of anaesthesia and when I came to, vomited immediately. That's normal, I was told, although nothing seemed normal. I didn't feel pain in my abdomen, but there wasn't pain before the miscarriage, either. The doctor told Tim that she'd removed a lot of "material," which lab tests later revealed to be a partial molar pregnancy.

According to the American Pregnancy Association website, there is no embryo in a molar pregnancy. Instead, the uterus fills with grape-like clusters of sacs called moles. In a partial molar pregnancy an embryo may be present at first, but it fails to develop and is soon overtaken by the growing moles. The cause of both conditions is genetic abnormality: the wrong number of chromosomes, which can occur through an error in cell division or when two sperm fertilize the same egg. Rarely, molar tissue may persist and lead to cancer. Molar pregnancy, also known as gestational trophoblastic disease—or more simply, a mole—affects approximately one in one thousand US pregnancies (the rate is higher in Mexico and parts of Asia). Partial molar pregnancy occurs less frequently. Twenty years ago, the dire sections of *What to Expect* gave no incidence rates. A short explanatory passage suggested that a fetus might survive partial molar pregnancy with a variety of abnormalities.

Standard treatment for a molar pregnancy is to eliminate it with a D&C. But afterward I began to worry that somehow I had consented to aborting a viable fetus, something I would not have done knowingly. My mind was fogged about whether there had been a long-odds chance for life—I didn't think so but later couldn't be sure. My confusion grew like uncontrollable moles taking over the space meant for a baby. But this was something I didn't discuss with the doctor. I felt too foolish, after the fact, to ask. It was an irrational preoccupation, surfacing at inopportune moments, nagging at me. I kept answering my own question with this: no heartbeat.

My little family of three carried on with our normal routine. Work got done, my husband and I were solid, and our daughter flourished. Sadness lingered, but I assigned it a physical cause: fluctuating hormones. I was weepy for weeks, empty and draggy. This period called to mind a phrase from AS Byatt's novel *Still Life*. Byatt's character Stephanie, heavily pregnant, is stuck in an hours-long queue to see her doctor, reading poetry to pass the time. She reads a few lines of Wordsworth that ordinarily would have lifted her heart, but they fail to move her, and so she realizes she is "sunk in biology." The idea is extended: "It was not a complaint. Biology was very interesting. She had never before imagined it could be so wholly voracious of time and attention." I, too, was sunk in biology in a different way: not expectantly, but in mourning, grieving without admitting it.

Yet it must, *must* be a sharper blow losing a baby if that baby is your first. The crib is empty; the preparations were for nothing. That has to be devastating, requiring a great force of will and love and hope to try again. After my pregnancy ended, I was thankful to have a child who made me laugh.

In October, just three months after the D&C, I found out that I was pregnant again. This time joy was tempered by fresh knowledge that a journey doesn't always end at the expected destination. Still, even though Tim and I now knew a couple of ways to get lost along the way (flawed personal data), this new start brought us happiness.

My doctor wasn't happy, though, far from it. She chastised me. We were supposed to wait; I was supposed to be examined in a follow-up visit to her office six weeks after the D&C and then, only then, might I be cleared for takeoff. But no one had told us this—not the doctor, and not her staff. No one had called to say it's time for your appointment and by the way, be careful not to conceive. Nor did they apologize for the oversight.

I should have left the practice right then but didn't. I stuck around, making nice, and the same doctor cared for me throughout the pregnancy. Only happenstance, a scheduling glitch, prevented her from delivering our second daughter, Sarah, in August 1995. Her on-call colleague attended the birth with cheery competence and no history with us.

Now I know, thanks to Dr. Wikipedia, that patients with partial molar pregnancies are advised to wait a year before becoming pregnant; they're supposed to be monitored regularly for signs of molar tissue still present, possibly spreading through the body. And for once, I'm thrilled to have been kept ignorant. I would not have wanted to brood about those facts while waiting for our Sarah to arrive. We coped with the worries we knew about, and then they faded as ultrasounds showed a beautiful growing baby, one who liked to kick and elbow me.

Examples of sadder circumstances than mine abound. A young friend has just lost a baby, her first, who only lived a few minutes after birth, and more than one relative has miscarried in the second trimester. The purpose of telling these stories is to share and make connections, but maybe not to compare pain levels. This isn't the heartbreak Olympics. I acknowledge, however, that women who have multiple miscarriages, who haven't been able to bring a baby to term, live with a heavier burden than someone like me. Nonetheless, my loss was more severe than I thought it would be; I tried to convince myself that I shouldn't feel sorrow, but I did.

Years passed, bringing another daughter, Madeleine, and then a son, Joseph, into our family. Soon I was well beyond the vice-grip of fertility, not even thinking about it. No longer worrying about keeping toddlers safe, fixated on looming adolescent problems. And then one day I realized that my period was late. Quite. Late. I began counting backwards and waited—two months, three. This is unbelievable, I thought, as I bought a pregnancy test—sneaking to another town for that purchase, hiding it like a teenager. I didn't feel pregnant; any number of factors could explain a menstrual pause. The results window of the test wand showed only a minus sign, never a plus. But still I waited and imagined the reaction of our teenagers if it turned out that I was expecting, ten years after the last child was born. Also: being the oldest mother at the playground, an unseemly mother, the most tired mother ever, and all the radical changes a new baby would bring. In truth, a hit of nostalgia also had me remembering the golden feeling of a babe in arms, the warm-skin bond of nursing, being needed more than anyone needs me now and wishing that would happen all over again. So when my period finally arrived, there was relief, but also bittersweet regret: I wasn't expecting, not this time and probably never again.

If asked by my children someday about my miscarriage, I'm not sure I'll be able to describe either the sadness or the love shot through that time. I'll probably fall back on pragmatism, advising them to collect as much information as they can, but not to put too much faith in it. Information is useful when it shows up at precisely the right time, but even then, key data will be missing. The pertinent facts may be revealed only after you needed them, or never, or you may misinterpret them.

Although there are days when I feel like a hardened veteran mama, I'm certainly no sage. Who am I to tell young women how to bear their losses? Yet I want to caution them, and my own daughters: the body knows. Life insists on itself, and sometimes it ends without warning. There is no way to prepare, no matter how much data you amass as a shield. Expect anything.

LAURA ROCK's fiction has appeared in Canadian publications including *The New Quarterly*, *U of T Magazine* (online), *The Antigonish Review*, and *The Dalhousie Review*, as well as the Irish journal *Southword*. One of her stories was awarded second prize in the 2011 Seán Ó Faoláin Short Story Prize competition. *The Globe and Mail* has published several of her essays. She lives in Lakefield, Ontario.

In This Kitchen

JENNIFER BOWERING DELISLE

"I'VE BEEN THINKING ABOUT it," Kent says, "and it feels like we are really close." I smile weakly. His voice is easy, light, as he drops the sidestripe shrimp that we bought from the boats in boiling water, their shells ticking against the side of the pot.

We have a rhythm in this kitchen, an unspoken knowing of who will chop and who will stand at the stove, a rhythm of bending sideways at the sink so the other can open the garbage cupboard, synchronizing fridge door and dishwasher door, here, taste this. We will peel the shrimp on our plates and dip them in warm lemon butter. I make salad: apple, bacon, pecans, the smell of toasting nuts filling the kitchen. What wine shall we open? I think there's a Gewürztraminer in the fridge. In these moments I almost feel human again, whole.

For two years I have been a walking uterus. Fallopian neck, my head full of eggs. I measure my life in months without names, twenty-eight days long. And every month my whole body bleeds, sheds its maternal potential. Empties.

We have been diagnosed with "unexplained infertility." "Diagnosed" doesn't seem like the right word, seems the opposite of "unexplained." After several tests the only thing the doctor can find wrong is that I have not carried a baby to term. The next step, he says, is to try a medicated intrauterine insemination, or IUI. I would take a drug called clomiphene to boost my ovulation, track my cycle by peeing on a stick every day and watching for the surge of hormones indicating I am about to ovulate, and then they would inject Kent's "washed" sperm into my uterus. Statistically, it would increase our chances of conceiving from three percent to ten percent. We think of it as science; perhaps it is just a different brand of luck.

We are feeding our child new foods. Tiny bites from our plates, of steak, of kale. He scrunches his face at the tastes he doesn't like, smears risotto across his high chair. We laugh, do you like it? He will like chocolate, like his mother, mango, like his father. A chubby fist wrapped around a spoon that is also a drumstick. Pasta sauce in his hair.

"There's nothing wrong with us," Kent is saying.

"That they could find."

"I'm not just being overly optimistic, I think we have a really good chance." He is pouring the pot of water into the sink, catching the bright shrimp in a colander.

"Just keep telling me that," I say, closing my eyes.

"This isn't just me trying to build you up."

"I know. It's you telling me you don't want to do the IUI yet."

"Not necessarily."

"I'm ready to try something else. I need to. I can't keep doing this month after month."

"I'm worried that if we do the IUI and it doesn't work, that you'll crash even harder."

"I worry about that too, but I also like the idea of giving up some of the control."

That first month we weren't pregnant the deep fear that I had always held since I first heard the word "infertile" burst to the surface. I knew it was irrational to expect to get pregnant the first try, but I could not help but imagine the worst. Every month I wasn't pregnant, I grieved. I grieved for the eggs that had fallen invisibly from my body. I grieved for the dreams I had since playing with dolls at three, of being a mother. Grieved for the children that were so clear in my mind, those scenes I could already see: picking her up when she falls in the playground, giving advice when his heart is broken. It was not absence, but loss. The thing that I had always wanted more than anything else, that others seemed to get so easily, seemed more distant, more blurry, with every month that passed.

Perhaps that deep fear came from some sort of internal knowing; perhaps it became a self-fulfilling prophecy. For the last two years I have Googled every twinge, I have counted the days in every phase of my cycle obsessively, worrying about my hormone levels, the thickness of my lining, the quality of my thirty-something-year-old eggs. I have spent hours reading online forums with posts by other panicking women suggesting green tea and pineapple core. I have taken my temperature and tracked my cervical mucous, and after ovulation I have analyzed the timing of our sex, the position. The clearer it became that getting pregnant was something I could not control, the more I have tried to control it. So there is comfort now in the notion of handing it over to a doctor and his syringe, of letting sex be sex and not a game that we keep losing.

"What if we have twins?" Kent asks. This is one of the risks of the medication.

"Then we'll figure it out. Maybe twins would be fun." I begin cutting up a baguette. He steals a piece. "I know it's not ideal," I say, "but it's time to take the next step. I need to feel like we're moving forward."

"But we know we can get pregnant."

The doctors use the word "spontaneous" for pregnancies achieved without medical intervention. "Spontaneous," almost like "immaculate," as if we looked at each other and conceived in an instant, with nothing but love. Perfect. As if the sixteen months of trying before we conceived were just a dream. I have never been as happy as I was then, imagining the baby growing inside me, imagining our family. I bought a baby names app for my phone and began suggesting names; Kent countered with silly suggestions: Guan-guan, Hat. We told a few friends and family, I had a T-shirt made for my brother's birthday that said UNCLE GRANT. At our first ultrasound the tech left the room without showing me the screen, without letting me hear the heartbeat. Telling me to get dressed and she would be right back. She came back after talking to a doctor hidden in a different room. "I could detect the pregnancy," she said, "but I think it's too early to get a proper measurement."

"But is it okay?"

"I think it's just too early."

I convinced myself over the next few days that she just had a lousy bedside manner. But when I saw my doctor the next week she frowned at the report. "I'm not sure how this is going to go," she said. It was too small, the heartbeat too weak. She gave the pregnancy a fifty-fifty chance. I had to return for another ultrasound in two weeks.

Those two weeks were like being underwater; we moved through our routines like walking on the bottom of the ocean. We stopped talking about names, about how to turn the office into a nursery. We did not breathe. On my laptop I still have the forum page bookmarked: "u/s found heartbeat but measuring small." Ten days later I began spotting, and I knew that it was over.

The miscarriage was not a unique loss. It was the culmination of sixteen months of loss. There were women online who had named their unborn embryos, whose signatures listed the dates of their losses alongside angel emoticons and declarations like "Gone but never forgotten" and "Mommy and Daddy Love You!" I couldn't feel this. I had been thrilled to be pregnant, I had wanted my child more than anything I had wanted before, but I could not think of it as a *child* that I had lost. I hadn't had the chance to begin to love it like a person and not an idea. I hadn't had the chance to hear a heartbeat, or see a grainy form on the ultrasound. In some strange way I envy these women this kind of grief. For even if it was fleeting, they had briefly been mothers.

We carry our food to the table, buoyed by the briny aroma of shrimp. We look down at our feast, cheers our wine glasses, good job team. We are neither of us technicians. We cook, but we don't bake. We never follow recipes. We prefer art over chemistry, even amateur, street-corner art. We like the romance of tasting, of making it up as we go, of making mistakes.

"It might not be easy for me to get away from work on the day you're ovulating."

"I know. If you have a meeting you can't get out of we'll just cancel it."

"I'll have to tell Bonnie. She'll need to know why I need to suddenly leave work to go masturbate."

"Is that how you'll tell her? Sorry Bonnie, I have to go masturbate."

"Yup. But seriously, she'll need to know. I can't just suddenly 'remember' I have a doctor's appointment that day."

"I hadn't thought of that." I don't want anyone to know. Even though everyone knows that we are trying since the miscarriage, I don't want the added pressure of friends and family wondering if our fertility treatments worked. "I guess we don't have a choice."

It has been six months now since I lost the baby. The fear that I may have another miscarriage has been drowned out by the fear that I will never even conceive again. The fear is like an electric current, pulsing through each cell, each capillary, each hair. It changes the way I touch the world—sparks when I touch cotton and light switches. In a few weeks I will mark the would-have-been due date. When you cannot conceive, the mourning of miscarriage does not end. Every month the bleeding is a renewal of that grief. Not because it is a reminder, but because it is the same.

I am watching Kent cook with our child. We have pulled a chair up to the counter for her to stand on; still she barely reaches his shoulder. She stirs awkwardly, but he is patient. He passes her an egg, lets her crack it against the bowl, laughs as he wipes the white from her tiny hands and picks the shards of shell out of the bowl. I can see it so clearly, those tiny hands in his.

The fertility specialist has given us a package of information, a prescription for the clomiphene, and a consent form. Within the legalese of the form I am "the patient," Kent just "the partner." "Please fill in your partner's information," it says, as though he is not one of the potential parents, as though he were not even in the room.

The nurse will hold me open with a speculum, swab my cervix with disinfectant, insert a catheter. I will lie on the table for five minutes to let the sperm find their way into my fallopian tubes. I will take Tylenol for the cramping. Seven days later I will have blood drawn to test my progesterone levels, seven days after that to test for the pregnancy hormone.

"I want to give you a baby, I don't want a doctor in a clinic to do it."

"It's still your sperm!"

"I know, but it's different. You will carry it for nine months. I only have a small part in this."

"But you will have a huge part in it. I'll need you to support me when I'm pregnant. You'll still be the father. You aren't 'giving me' a baby. It will be our child."

He looks down at the food on the table, at this meal we have made together. This is not the way it is supposed to be. Our love was supposed to be enough to make our family. "I don't want to *bake* a baby, I want to cook a baby."

"Don't tell anybody else you want to cook a baby," I laugh. But I am crying too. He is thinking not of what we might gain but of what else we have to lose.

Our list of losses is long. But I have learned where to file them. I will never again tell my parents for the first time that they are going to be grandparents. That memory is now forever bitter. But on the list that print is so fine, so faint. Crowding out all the other words on the page is the child that does not yet exist, the fear that he or she may never exist.

We want to make the choice rationally, we do not want to be manipulated by fear into acting rashly, into doing an unnecessary procedure. But perhaps I should not think of fear as being the opposite of reasonableness. Perhaps we need the fear to make it clear what we need to do. To make it clear what is most important to us. To make it clear how far we will be willing to go.

I had always imagined that first moment, taking a pregnancy test and looking at it with my husband, our eyes wide in amazement and joy. I could taste it. The outer skin of the dream is now shrivelled and bruised. But the core of it remains, the heart.

I am lying with my daughter on her bed, reading a story. I am sitting with my son in the sand at the beach. A face with Kent's eyes, my round chin. "Where do babies come from?"

"Let me tell you," I say. "Let me tell you how much you were wanted."

We pile the food onto our plates, this meal that we have made, and begin to peel the shrimp in front of us, juice running down our arms. They are full of tiny bright red eggs.

JENNIFER BOWERING DELISLE has published poetry, non-fiction, and fiction in a variety of literary journals, and is a member of the editorial collective of *Room Magazine*. She holds a PHD in Canadian literature from the University of British Columbia. She lives in Edmonton.

THE WOUNDED PAST
CANNOT DENY THE
BEAUTIFUL FUTURE

The Fragmentary Blue
of a Butterfly

KEVIN BRAY

I HAVE LITTLE FAITH in slim chances, especially about the likelihood of a sunny day on a summer weekend, just as I have little trust in the men and women who run my pension plan and who tell me the forecasts for future endowments and unfunded liabilities. I have learned through experience and theory that much of life is too complex to be foretold, that predictions are intemperate, that John Lennon might have known something about chaos theory when he wrote that "life is what happens to you while you're busy making other plans." The best laid plans of mice and men often go awry and a slight change in the wind can set your ship off course forever. You end up in America, not India, or you end up in church in October getting married rather than in journalism school in September.

I was twenty-five and she was twenty-three when we married. We were below the average age for most informed adults who forthrightly proclaim the (statistically improbable) promise of lifetime fidelity and love. The circumstance of our lives comprised a textbook portrait found in sociology courses. We had both lost parents, suffered varied abuses as children, ignored the calamitous events that befell us while dating (even now I cannot bring myself to openly write about them). We were doomed from the moment the rings were bought, but we were young and raw. We believed hope and possibility might rescue us. There are so few colours in the emotional rainbow when you are young and you honestly think that grey will never obscure the pot of gold.

In our first apartment my wife and I chose a black and white decorating scheme. It was simple: buy pieces of each non-colour and with enough opposing elements you could find a balance. It was a sage and practical demonstration that opposites attract and it offered a constant overt reminder that harmony was merely the addition of positive and negative, black and white, yin and yang. This lasted only a year. The monochromatic scheme was so uninteresting, so contrived and constraining. We struggled with colours for another ten years, going so far as to hire a decorator for the last house we owned, the one that I walked around at night asking myself if I was prepared to lose it and the life attached to it. In the family room of this house I applied a deep red paint, the kind you see in the estate homes of rich people whose equine children are immortalized in paintings above the fireplace. It was called "Caliente," meaning spicy and stimulating (Benjamin Moore avoids paint chip names that stir unsettled thoughts). I wrote REDRUM on the walls in wide brush strokes, thinking it was funny. After I was done rolling the walls, you could faintly see the ridges of the brushed letters below the smoother tracks of the roller. There was no murderous intent on anyone's life, just my own.

I never wanted children, or a child. For years I cultivated a creation myth about writers and therefore about myself in which all writers had their genesis in solitude and penury, or if they had an income and spouse, then at least they had significant hours for seclusion and scribbles. Let me be clear that I did not write, although I wrote a few sentences, really good ones I think. I took a writing course with a mid-list Canadian writer and felt that her encouraging comments on a draft could be the fuel that fired my rocket into the literary constellation. Nothing came of this. My writing sputtered when a heartbroken friend moved in with us after a righteous break-up. For two weeks my wife and I hospitably honoured his grief while I wrote nothing. He moved out and on and six years passed without another word from me. In 1997 I started a correspondence course with Timothy Findley (I sent my work to France where he lived in Cotignac and he replied with—typed!—letters and a cordial signature—so much better than the Internet interlocution offered today). Of course, the sand pile of my life, the tiny grains deposited daily, was forming a tall cone and the angle of repose—the angle beyond which one more grain of sand would collapse the entire edifice—was near. The accretion of sand is the collection of moments and minutes, good and bad, circumstance and happenstance, and no one can predict the exact moment that the pile will fall.

It collapsed when my wife was pregnant. Intellectually I knew that a child would arrive in nine months, less if you start the clock on the day the doctor confirms. Humans have an amazing adaptive response to an incipient crisis: denial and ignorance. I subsumed my anxiety-on-the-cusp-of-panic within my writing, which was insipid and intermittent. In nine months (the irony is not lost) I sent four letters to Findley and received four replies. At the same time I was behaving like an inglorious bastard, looking for an improvised explosive device that could blow apart the marriage and free me from fatherhood.

Hours before my daughter was delivered by Caesarean section, I sat in the hospital cafeteria writing in my journal. My entry for that early morning, two coffees after midnight, was about her name and its meaning. Months before, I'd written a short story about a woman whose daughter drowns in the ocean; the mother swims far out to sea every afternoon, searching for some sign of her missing child. I named the mother Chloe. This was not a portent of bad things—I just liked the sound of the name and wanted to create someone noble and pure called Chloe. In my journal I told my future daughter what her name meant in Greek mythology and then appended an explanation for her middle name, which is Hope. Findley had liked the story, "partly for that careful incompleteness — for the fact that we don't know exactly what will become of Chloe. We get to write that, ourselves."

Chloe came into the home three days after birth and I left the home six weeks after her arrival. I found an apartment five minutes away and returned to the family home every night for a few hours to help with our baby. On weekends I came over for most of the day. A taut filament of shared responsibility for Chloe kept mother and father together for these hours, and six months later when Chloe's mother returned to work I would spend three nights a week sleeping on the sofa of her apartment (we had by now sold the matrimonial residence) and stagger to my daughter's crib at 2:00 AM with a warm bottle.

I remember one evening, roughly halfway between what should have been eight hours of sleep, holding Chloe against my chest and looking out on lamplight through which snowflakes as large as feathers floated down to the ground. It was so quiet that it felt like I had lost my hearing and I hummed a little James Taylor to reconnect with the space around us. I was still not writing, although I now had two journals to use as records of Chloe's presence; one was used to catch moments and the other was used to write letters to her (she is fifteen now and I will give the journals to her in a few years). We had a video camera, but unedited film becomes as boring as a red-light camera, recording the mundane comings-and-goings of everyday happenings, so I wrote the things I felt and heard, thinking that this held greater verisimilitude.

I could not send these to Findley. I was supposed to be working on a few stories that he'd reviewed, but fathering (so different from mere parenting) and separating had expunged whatever creativity I might muster. Any words in the creativity hopper were reserved for the Chloe letters, or recording the daily Chloe news, where I scribbled just a little outside the lines when I interpreted her gestures or expressions (*she must love me*, I would think). I sent Findley a Coles Notes update on my marital imbroglios, and he responded kindly with "I hope that all works out for you for the best with your family situation, and I hope, even more, that you persist with the writing."

My daughter Chloe was seven years old when I witnessed chaos theory. She had begged to have her hair braided by one of the women who walk up and down the beaches of Paradise Island in the Bahamas. For a little fortune, we purchased fifteen rows of braids. The woman sat her bags of baubles and brushes with my daughter on the pie-warm sand, just above the watermark of the last wave, and started threading Chloe's hair into strands that were quickly laced and beaded. To do it right, she had to tug on my daughter's head and cinch the braids, hard and painful enough that Chloe tried to distract herself by grabbing fistfuls of sand and dropping them into a pile. As the braiding continued, the pile of sand grew into an inverted cone, mathematically precise in its dimensions and simultaneously Chloe made little sniffling noises, precursors to a larger, racking sobbing. The sand cone piled higher, each dilation preserving its numerical commonsense and then, when I was sure that Chloe would break from the incessant tugging and increasing pain, the cone collapsed and the final bead was threaded.

Chloe's emotional state and the pile of sand are what mathematicians call "nonlinear systems." They're like the stock market, or the weather, or anything else that teases us with a hint of predictability. I could tell that one small sniffle would follow the next one, but I couldn't know if the sniffles would suddenly cascade into a torrent of tears. I could reasonably assume that the next handful of sand would extend the cone, but didn't know when the entire shape would collapse into the beach. Complex things, like human emotions, or weather, or sand castles, exist on the edge of structure and order and can swiftly descend into uncontrollable, chaotic conclusions. A butterfly beats its wings and the barely perceptible turbulence of this act sets in motion a twirling vortex that creates a hurricane; a stock sale by one seller in one city on one day leads to a panic sell-off and a plunge in the Dow Jones; a piece of toast burns and two minutes are lost in the morning routine, leading later in the day to a horrific car crash. Chaos surrounds us, ready to disassemble lives, and if we ignore its precepts we never feel the fragmentary blue of a butterfly as it passes.

It is Friday, October 13, 1964. The road is straight, the weather is fine, and the pavement is dry and untarnished. The white dotted line that keeps vehicles apart through the power of suggestion is visible. Cars drive past a particular marker on the Trans-Canada in staccato rhythm and each car leaves a grain of sand on the pile as it passes. The cone grows taller and wider until my father's car and another car, coming from the opposite direction, deposit their grains and the angle of repose is revealed. Whose grain has collapsed the pile is irrelevant. My father is killed with the hitchhiker he has picked up, a young man returning from a funeral where he was a pallbearer. Five people are killed in the other car. A blue butterfly is thrown from its flight path by the shock wave of sound when metal torques into lethal bends and it beats its wings harder to compensate. A tiny breeze is born. A thousand lives will be changed.

I am stolen from my mother (I am three and a half years old) by a well-intentioned aunt and my sister is stolen by a different aunt. We will be raised apart, forever. My new mother decides that I need a new sister and adopts a baby girl who will grow up to look for and find her mother and the sister she never knew. My birth mother, who has lost everything, will leave Canada and return only when her son is a grown man. She keeps her married name so that he can one day find her and because someone has created the Internet, he will. He does this with the help of a woman he meets online, a circumstance that can only transpire after he has left his wife and spent a few years as a single dad in an emotional vacuum that his human nature abhors. But he abandoned his marriage because the concentric and widening circles of emotional damage that ripple out from the first stone thrown—the death of his father—make him unsuitable for commitment. (In some oddly justifiable way, he decides that if he is going to be a parent then he wants a daughter, but it takes his psychiatrist to square the circle of life and reveal that Chloe cannot be recompense for his childhood losses.) His second father dies and is buried with his first father and because some people think of him as a writer, he will write the eulogy. He delivers this eulogy on an October afternoon that is riven by rain and wind. No one else beside the grave can see grains of sand dropping onto a larger pile of sand in front of the headstone. There is a possible narrative line, but he can't see it because just when the arc is revealed a tiny wing flutters and the line disappears into a circle into the whirlpool of his life.

Rich Western societies have created a storyline for life that is wishfully predictive. There is a life cycle for every facet of us. We are spenders and savers and income earners and income burners over different subsets of financial life. Like time-lapse photography that shows the growth and demise of a plant, we can be animated in film to show the rise and fall of our bodies in an expected pattern that none of us will escape. We expect freedom at fifty-five, seven careers, two marriages, maybe one child, and a top-three disease to finish us off at the end of the gender-specific allowance for living. There are seven habits that bestow effectiveness (highly effective people have no time for eight), five stages of grief, five layers in Maslow's hierarchy. None of this matters. The tiniest shift in your life, or a slight perturbation in the orbit of someone outside your constellation of friends and family, can deliver a tornado to your door and destroy the facade you built. There are no stages or stairs in a world created by chaos.

No one will escape chaos. There is nothing in books that can help you avoid or subjugate the butterfly effect. There are butterflies everywhere. Birth is a metamorphosis. Your child enters the world and everything you expected is no longer possible. Books offer no equation that can resolve the wild outcomes created by the beating of a baby's heart. I could not forecast my future or speculate that one day I would be making dinner while my daughter sat on the edge of the kitchen sink with her little feet splashing in the basin and we would sing Raffi songs.

Until I became a father I had adhered to the poet Stephen Spender's lament and acquiescence contained in "What I Expected." His first stanza resonated with me as I was spending a lot of time rock climbing, a cliché for sure as I hung onto the limestone cliffs while my everyday ordinary life offered no purchase.

> What I expected, was
> Thunder, fighting,
> Long struggles with men
> And climbing.

I still have long struggles with foes unseen and unpredictable, but the wounded past cannot deny the beautiful future, if it is at all possible. All the mathematics in the world, every equation I might construct, every coin I could flip, will not yield an expectation of anything other than "que sera, sera." Plan if you must, but do not imperil yourself with heartache and disappointment by spending too much time reading prescriptive books on a summer's day while a butterfly alights on your beach towel.

KEVIN BRAY lives in Toronto and teaches (for money), writes (for non-pecuniary reasons), and blogs (for resolution). He spent a few months back in the late 1990s working with Timothy Findley at the Humber School for Writers. You can find some of Bray's work in *The Globe and Mail*, *The Healing Muse*, *Airplane Reading*, and *The Barnstormer*.

Female Troubles

SUSAN OLDING

THE BAY CENTRE FOR Birth Control is a small, squat building made of yellow brick. It sits back from the road, behind a stamp-sized yard, dwarfed and doomed by the gleaming towers that surround it on all sides. An unforgiving sun pricks my scalp as I tramp across the pathway to its frosted glass door. My boyfriend leans against the low stone wall near the street, whistling under his breath.

The waiting room is tiny, bare except for banners advertising International Women's Day and some other feminist festivals. A large chart lists the names and failure rates of various contraceptive devices. No safe sex posters here. This is the seventies, before we knew about HIV and AIDS, when the worst consequences of sex were unwanted pregnancies, botched abortions, broken hearts.

My feet itch in their canvas platform espadrilles and the waistband of my pale green polyester dress pinches my skin. I chose this dress especially for the trip from the suburbs to the city. After my appointment, Paul and I plan to walk north, toward Bloor Street. We are going out to dinner in Yorkville. Before boarding the commuter train, we studied the newspaper to find out about the latest restaurants, and that same paper, the *Star*, was also my guide for information about this clinic. The article I read was reassuring. I know they will dispense pills to girls my age without their parents' permission.

A harried young doctor leads me to an examining room and asks how she can help. Her eyes sweep across the table with its shiny metal stirrups, then linger on the shelf behind it as she calculates whether or not she has everything she'll need for the obligatory pelvic exam. But today there will be no internal exam. As I bend to reach into my purse, marbles of sweat bounce down my spine. I pull a pink plastic packet out of a side compartment and show it to her.

"What's this? This is the pill, isn't it. It's not some kind of mini-pill. It will stop me from getting pregnant?"

"Of course." She hands it back, her expression bemused. "Where did you get it?"

I got it from Dr. Fernwood, my mother's gynecologist. Some months ago we went together to visit him. I had been suffering from painful periods. My friends' doctors had given them codeine or extra-strength Aspirin for the same complaint; I wanted something similar. While my mother sat smoking in the next room, I primly explained to Dr. Fernwood (an old friend and colleague of my doctor father, a frequent guest at my parents' parties) that I did not want to go on the pill. I wasn't sexually active and I didn't want to take hormones. I'd been reading *Ms.* and *Our Bodies, Ourselves* and had a well-developed horror of the reputed side effects.

Dr. Fernwood ignored me. He lied. "This isn't the same as the pill," he said, his familiar voice smooth and buttery as an avocado. "Very low, very low, low dosage. And it will help you with those cramps of yours. Guaranteed."

I had to admit, it did help. Later, I discovered my mother had put him up to it, had in fact insisted on this duplicitous course of treatment. She was scared I had started having sex, she told me. And although in our many conversations about this subject, she had always maintained that she'd support me, *no matter what*, in the end, the risk that I might become pregnant proved impossible to accept. Maybe she just wanted to protect me, to prevent all my fine opportunities from vanishing down a diaper pail.

Eventually, of course, Paul and I did decide to have sex. But I had taken my mother's hidden message much to heart, and although I was curious, even eager, my passion for research was more powerful. I skimmed my father's medical journals, scanned them for ads. Dr. Fernwood's pill must have been a relatively new brand, because I had to plow through three or four glossy issues of the *New England Journal of Medicine* before I found its name. Still, at last, there it was—the soft-focus photograph of the pretty, carefree woman in flowing skirts, the swirling, blurry background of purple and gold, and in the fine print on the facing page, amid an alarmingly long list of precautions and contraindications, the magic words I was searching for: *estradiol*, and *progesterone*, and mostly: *oral contraceptive*.

Even then, I was not content. "I know what it is," I said. "But I'd still like to check, just to be certain."

"Sure," Paul agreed, good-natured as always.

That young doctor must have enjoyed a long, lusty laugh with her friends after her shift was over. But for now she calmly cuffed me, measured my blood pressure, listened for a minute to my heart. "Well," she said. "Seeing as it's already been prescribed, and you've come all this way, I might as well give you a few samples." She thrust the pastel packets into my hands like penny candy. "Just make sure you take it at the same time every day. No forgetting."

Vindicated, relieved, triumphant, I fairly skipped down the path as I left the clinic. There, on the buzzing street, under the indifferent glare of the glass office towers, Paul and I giggled and kissed.

"Probably it's all for nothing anyway," I joked, as we began our trek toward Bloor Street. "Probably I'm not even capable of having kids."

"Oh, come off it," he said. "Of course you are."

That's how careful I was. That's how seriously I took the word "precautions." How strong my need was to control my own life, every moment, every breath of it. How deep my faith that such a thing was possible.

Barren: Of a woman: incapable of bearing children; infertile.

For the past three years, my husband and I have been trying to conceive a child. Coincidentally, during these same years, I've had problems with my periods. Heavy flow. Strange aches. My doctor is affiliated with the local teaching hospital, and for two consecutive visits I am seen by residents when I report for my annual Pap smear. "Do you think I might have fibroids or endometriosis?" I ask the first one. "Oh, no." She shuffles through my file. "That's unlikely." The second reassures me: "It's normal to get a change in your periods as you age. Nothing's wrong."

This year, Mark is on sabbatical and I have taken a leave from my job to write a novel. We are living in another part of the country. An unusually early period sends me to a doctor here. He listens to my story and then somewhat reluctantly signs the order for a sonogram. "It might be a fibroid," he says. "But even if it is, there's nothing we can do. Hysterectomy. That's it. And if you're trying to get pregnant . . ." He shrugs. "It's not really an option, is it."

No.

I prepare by drinking a litre of water. In radiology, the technician slaps pale green gel onto my distended abdomen. "You're too full," she says. "I'll let you go in just a second." But she doesn't. The instant the white plastic probe makes contact with my skin, something strange leaps into view. Turning away from the frown suddenly creasing her forehead, I force myself to breathe. *What if . . . what if, by some miracle, I am pregnant?* But that's silly. I know I'm not. My period is due in three days, and already my breasts are swollen and tender, already I feel the usual tugs and stirrings, so different, I imagine, from the tugs and stirrings of new life.

The machine talks to itself in bleeps as the technician probes my belly. I wince. Normally, I tolerate pain quite well, am good at relaxing into it, but this hurts, it hurts a *lot*, and I can't pretend. "I'll let you go in a second," she repeats. "Afterwards, come back. We'll need to take more pictures."

I peer into the monitor. There it is again, that strange swelling. She presses and it jumps closer, filling the screen. Two black spots cloud its centre, blurry around the edges like a pair of thick-lashed eyes. It looks like a baby seal.

"Have you ever taken follicle-stimulating drugs?"

I stammer, stupid with confusion. "Folic. Follicle? I've been taking folic acid. But that's not the same. Is it."

"No, that's not the same," she agrees, without looking at me.

When my parents were newly married, my father was still in medical school and unable to support a child. Then, when he began his residency, they decided it was time to start a family. My mother tells me she had some trouble getting pregnant. In the language of the day, her uterus was "tipped." Supposedly, this made things more difficult. "We'd given up," she says. "I thought it wasn't going to happen."

"Then what?"

"Then . . . well . . . it did. But at first, I couldn't believe it. When I missed my period, I got scared. I thought there must be something wrong. It had to be something wrong. I thought you . . . I thought you were a tumour."

Of an animal: not pregnant at the usual season.

The first time I had unprotected sex I was thirty-two years old. I was premenstrual that night and so knew the odds of pregnancy were next to nil. In my twenties, I was ambivalent about having children, financially and emotionally unstable, unsure of my capacity to mother. At around thirty, I began to feel more confident that I could parent, but my first marriage floundered and then ended, and the relationship I entered afterwards was in its early years, too improbable, too provisional to shelter a new life. And so I waited. In this I was not alone. None of my university-educated friends had children, either. All led similar lives; all asked themselves similar questions, interrogating their own fears and longings over and over again. We were the first generation never to have known a world without the pill, and the pill—whether we took it or not—drastically altered our experience, separating us from our mothers and even from our older cousins and sisters.

This year, my friends and acquaintances are having babies. A colleague my age, who miscarried last year, brings her next child to term and after a long and difficult labour, successfully delivers a son. Two of my best friends announce their pregnancies within weeks of each other; another gives birth to her second daughter. My husband, who has grown children from his previous marriage, discovers himself a young grandfather. In this unusually early spring, a season of almost embarrassing abundance, I see pregnant women and babies everywhere—on the street, in the supermarket lineup, at the doctor's office, in my dreams.

"Technically, of course," my gynecologist says, "the best time to get pregnant is when you're sixteen or seventeen. It may not be the best time socially, but biologically . . ." His voice trails off. He is a few years younger than I am, not long out of medical school. Last week, he postponed our appointment because he had to stay home to care for his newborn twins. While we talk, he doodles on the pad in front of him. I can see the logo: a pharmaceutical firm based in my hometown. They manufacture birth control pills and spermicidal jelly. "We'll see what we can do," he finally says.

Of a tree or plant: not producing fruit or seed.
I have a fibroid, Dr. Cooper tells me, a benign uterine tumour. Not uncommon, not ordinarily dangerous, but in my case, because of its size and location, a possible cause of infertility, since it appears to be irritating a portion of the uterine wall and may also be compressing the fallopian tubes. This fibroid, however, is the least of my worries. I also have a large ovarian cyst. It could be a normal, follicular cyst; then again, it could be an endometrioma, or perhaps it is a benign dermoid cyst; possibly it is cancerous. He will have to run more tests; I'll need another ultrasound.

If the cyst is not the normal, follicular type, the doctor says, I may not be releasing eggs at all. Or the eggs I do release may be unhealthy, incapable of implanting themselves in my already inflamed endometrial wall. On the other hand, they may implant themselves, but briefly, so that I miscarry at the very moment I would expect my period to arrive.

"It may be coming out in the wash," he explains. "So to speak."

Of land: producing little vegetation; unproductive.
Since my first appointment with the gynecologist, I am finding it difficult to work. Every morning I go to my desk and switch on the computer; every evening I glance through my notebook and read the sketches and bits of scenes I've compiled for the novel I am writing. On the days when I manage to immerse myself in my imaginary world, work is a wonderful distraction. But most days, my characters remain as distant as they were before I dreamed them. Most days, I have trouble making myself care about mere words.

I surf the Internet instead. There are many, many "resources" for infertile couples. Doctors' home pages, links to Britain and Australia, books, chat lines and support groups, descriptions and fee schedules for the expensive, controversial assisted reproductive technologies. I find it overwhelming. One source tells me that at least a sixth of North American couples experience infertility, medically defined as the inability to conceive after a year of unprotected intercourse. Thirty-five percent of the cases are "female factor" (the woman's fault, I can't help thinking), thirty-five percent are "male factor" (how neat and equal, that division!). In twenty percent of cases, both people have some difficulty, and the rest are "unexplained."

From what I understand, each of us responds to this condition differently. Each has her own ways of accommodating to it—or not. But in general, our emotions are predictable. Shock, denial, guilt, rage, blame, bargaining, jealousy, depression—the usual catalogue of grief.

"My life is meaningless without children," a woman says. "I am afraid my husband will divorce me," says another.

One fertility specialist in Atlanta almost seems to relish these expressions of despair for the contrast they provide to his eventual "happy endings." Dr. Perloe's laudable aim is to transform his patients from victims and "guinea piggies" into active participants in their treatment. Chapters in his online book include advice on "developing an individualized plan" and becoming "a positive force in your own fertility treatment." Yet despite the exhaustive and accurate information it contains, despite its upbeat slogans and its rhetoric of agency and control, his book is at bottom a fairy tale. The title, *Miracle Babies*, betrays its true genre. In it, Perloe plays the roles of wizard and prince, creating life where none was possible before, restoring the virtuous, who work and wait, to their illusion that they can do whatever they dream.

Well. Why not? He and other doctors like him *are* making people happy. Some of his patients get pregnant; some of the couples in his book are raising their children as I write. And however skeptical I feel, the stories tempt me. Reading them, I wonder: *What if?* Three years ago, the prospect of in vitro fertilization would have moved me to sputter and choke; now I consider it an option, and for a fee of just over four thousand dollars, worth every penny at the price.

Why do I want a child? Why does anyone? One friend, not to our knowledge infertile but as a lesbian unsure as yet whether she'll become a parent, describes the almost "reptilian" ache she feels when she cradles someone's baby. "It's not jealousy," another, possibly infertile friend insists. "Truly, it's not. But it makes me horribly sad."

I do not want a child to carry on the family name or the family business. I do not want a child to complete me or transform me into an adult. I do not need a child to look up to me now or look after me in old age. I want a child because finally, in my thirties, I have learned a few things about love and how to share it. I want a child because, together, Mark and I would be good parents. That is all.

Destitute of interest or attraction; arid; dull.

What must it have been like, one hundred, two hundred years ago or more, to carry the label "barren"? Some of those women lost their heads if they had the misfortune to marry a king. Some, taken for witches, were burned. Some burned inside for shame, having failed to fulfill God's purpose. And others, with what sweet relief, must have tossed aside their stays, freed as no one else was to be sexual, to lie with a man in hot embrace, unafraid of the childbed's fierce exhaustions and grave dangers.

These days, infertility ruins more sex lives than it enhances. I hear about people who blame their own bodies, who feel cheated and undone by their own flesh. I read about couples who pick fights as a way of avoiding "sex on demand," couples who fake the X's in their basal body temperature charts, lying to their doctors, lying to themselves.

This does not happen to Mark and me. Perhaps because, until now, we had no reason to suspect an ovulatory dysfunction and so have not been keeping strict records, together we look forward to the peak time of the month, make trying a kind of game. But when I first hear the word "hysterectomy," as applied to me, something inside me falters. I picture my mother's friends, who had this operation twenty years ago, and remember them as impossibly old. In fact, they *were* older than I am now, but not by so many years. I begin to notice—with such pangs!— each new grey hair, each tiny line. And then, after my first sonogram, the image of my "growths" feels inscribed into my brain, and when Mark leans over to touch me, I seem to feel their swelling more insistently.

I walk to the beach near our temporary home. The day is warm and clear, and the sand is crowded with sunbathers. Next to me lie two lovers, as entangled as the wild roses lining the path, her pretty brown calf slung across his hip, his dark head nestled into the crook of her silver-bangled arm. *Unfair, unfair,* I want to shout at them. I think of Roethke's line about a woman lovely in her bones, and wonder when, or if, that liquid sensuality will ever return to me; when, or if, I will ever again feel a glow, like pollen, beneath my skin.

Producing no result; fruitless; unprofitable.

The blood test is negative. I don't have cancer. The second sonogram is a success. My cyst has disappeared.

Mark and I perch on a hospital cot to hear the news. Dr. Cooper sits below us in his sea-green surgical scrubs, a smile animating his freckled face. "I'll be honest with you," he says. "I didn't think it was going to turn out like this. I thought we were going to have to do surgery right away. That first ultrasound didn't look good."

In his relief, which is almost as pronounced as our own, he forgets for a minute that the "fertility issue" has yet to be resolved. Because even as it demonstrates that my cyst was of the normal, follicular type, even as it reveals my perfectly ordinary ovaries, the second ultrasound also illuminates the fibroid. Still there, still growing, still a possible culprit in our failure to conceive.

"What are the options for treatment?" Mark wonders.

"Not great," the doctor admits.

Hysterectomy, the traditional solution, must for obvious reasons be ruled out. There are drugs designed to shrink the tumour, but they are too powerful to take for any longer than six months, and their major side effect is unpleasant—an instant (if temporary) menopause, abrupt and for many women psychologically overwhelming, not least because it is counterintuitive. Menopause ordinarily marks the end of a woman's fertile years, so it is far from easy to accept this passage as fertility's potential beginning. Then, too, the drugs are expensive—about four hundred and fifty dollars a month, not covered by health insurance— quite a hefty price to pay for almost certain discomfort and an entirely uncertain result. Finally, apart from drug therapy, the only option is myomectomy, a surgical procedure to remove the fibroid. This carries all the risks of any major surgery, and as with the drugs, can at best be considered a temporary solution, since whichever course of treatment is chosen the fibroid will likely grow back within six months.

"You'd have a three- or four-month window of opportunity," Dr. Cooper says. "Three or four months to get pregnant. That's it. Then you'd be back where you started from."

The cost of infertility treatments can be enormous. Some people spend more than thirty thousand dollars in their efforts to conceive a child. They borrow from relatives or friends, take out second or third mortgages, factor the price of drugs into their monthly budgets along with food and rent and other necessities. And to what avail? According to RESOLVE, an infertility advocacy group, while the spontaneous conception rate for those who go untreated for infertility is only five percent, among those who seek treatment, almost fifty percent eventually succeed in conceiving. But those figures express generalizations. The success of treatment depends on the specific problem being addressed, as well as on the woman's health and age. Statistics are often misleading applied to my own situation, or yours.

And what of the social costs? The reluctance of public and private insurers to pay the bills for some procedures may be justified. An Indian source puts it most starkly: "There are already too many babies in this country. Why exacerbate the population problem by producing more?" Doctors Anjali and Aniruddha Malpani, the authors of *Getting Pregnant– A Guide for the Infertile Couple* and themselves infertility specialists, argue on the contrary that each of us has a "biological right" to have a child, and the fact that our neighbours may have "too many" children is no reason to deny us our own. Moreover, infertility treatments are a "much more cost-effective use of resources than a number of other accepted surgical procedures," such as kidney transplants or joint replacements, they claim. No one objects to heart surgery for a seventy-year-old man whose life expectancy is only a few more years. Why cavil, then, over a few hundred or even a few thousand dollars spent to address the health needs of people in their thirties, who have their entire lives ahead of them?

But not everyone agrees with the fertility doctors, of course. And those of us without children may be excused for a hint of bitterness about that. For whether we choose our childless condition or not, we risk the appellation "selfish." Meanwhile, the assisted reproductive technologies should make social and ethical theorists of us all. Reports of high-risk multiple births and of doctors or technicians inseminating patients with their own sperm, taking eggs and embryos without their patients' consent, or exploiting their patients with expensive, unsuitable, and often damaging treatments percolate in the media and in our collective imagination. Is this the kind of world we want to live in? Is this the kind of world anybody's children deserve?

Of a person: unresponsive; dull.

Infertility is not a subject many people know how to talk about. While the difference in our ages and the existence of Mark's grown children protect us from the crudely jovial ("About time you two started a family!"), even some of my closest friends turn insensitive when faced with this trouble they don't share. "Maybe it's for the best," one insists. "This way, you'll do more writing. Give birth to books." "But that isn't how you define yourself," another reminds me. "You have so many other roles. You don't really *need* to be a mother."

And it's true. I am lucky. In an unmarried aunt who worked, travelled the world, and never left off learning, I have always had a model of one way to live a childless life. I love and am loved by a good man, a man who knows how to talk, and who, more than that, knows how to listen. Living with him these past eight years, I have watched his children blossom and thrive partly as a result of my care, and my work as a teacher gives me further opportunities to counsel, encourage, and nurture. Finally, I have solid, sustaining friendships with women, the dearest of whom is a poet who has chosen to remain childless—meaning I never need to fear that children will be all she wants to talk about; meaning words, my first and most enduring love, will always find an echo.

Yet none of this erases my desire to bear and raise my own child. No matter how I look at it, infertility is a loss, a painful, too private bereavement. How am I to mourn for something that never was? How grieve for what might have been, for what could have, would have, should have?

My fourteen-year-old cat is a lifelong asthmatic. Recently, his condition worsened, and I thought he was going to die. Lying beside him on the bed, listening for hours to the rattle in his lungs, then driving blindly to the vet's, sure that each weak gasp might be his last, I had a dim presentiment of the kind of pain a parent feels, forced to watch her own child suffer. Then, with treatment, Sid's health began by slow degrees to improve, and holding him purring in my arms, or watching him extend one delicate dark paw in a patch of sunlight on the carpet, I drew a breath of the pure, sweet joy, of the incandescent euphoria that must rise inside a mother whenever she catches her own child unawares and is permitted, for that instant, simply to see her as she is—separate, unique, a whole and perfect self.

There is nothing duller than death, nothing more barren than a grave. We do not like to be reminded of infertility because like any condition that cannot be cured, like any disease that can't be beaten, like death itself, it is permanent, and like death itself, it is ultimately out of our control. The Bay Centre for Birth Control was torn down many years ago, and in its place, one block west, the offices of the "miracle baby" doctors line the gleaming hospital towers. But we are all of us getting older, and all of us, all of us will die, and even our children and our carefully crafted books will only outlast us a little while.

SUSAN OLDING is the author of *Pathologies: A Life in Essays*, winner of the Creative Nonfiction Collective's Readers' Choice Award for 2010. Her poetry and prose have appeared widely in literary journals, magazines, and anthologies across Canada and the United States, including *Event*, the *Los Angeles Review of Books*, *The Malahat Review*, and the *Utne Reader*. She has been a finalist for a National Magazine Award, two Western Magazine Awards, and a CBC Literary Award, and she is the recipient of a number of prizes and honours, including the Brenda Ueland Prose Prize for Literary Non-fiction and *The New Quarterly*'s Edna award. Born in Toronto, she currently lives with her family in Kingston.

Invisible Mending

FIONA TINWEI LAM

I

In the palliative care ward, my brother and I watched my sister bathe our mother's body one last time before it was transported to the funeral home. Our mother had died a few hours before, at 3:00 AM. This was the first time I had seen her naked since my childhood. Although she was seventy-four years old, her body seemed oddly young and slim. The weight she'd gained over the last decade while living in care homes had melted away during the weeks in palliative care. She'd never had more than laugh crinkles and deep smile or frown folds on either side of her mouth, and now as she lay prone on the bed, the skin of her face was utterly smooth. I stood by her feet, looking at her body, which was so similar to mine in shape, yet tinier, more delicate. I could see the faint traces of the cumulative stretch marks on her belly from bearing the three of us. My brother stood beside her, close to the faint seam of her Caesarean scar where he'd entered the world. We three stood at closed portals, as if death had severed some invisible umbilical cord, one that had tethered us to her all our lives. We were now afloat and adrift, uprooted and unanchored from her life, her history, her memories. In birth as in death we were here in hospital with our mother, coming full circle. I felt the shift viscerally: we had become the roots and anchors for the next generation.

Her presence had fled the room hours before, following an afternoon and evening of hoarse panting that had come on suddenly, as if she were running the last leg of a marathon, straining to reach that finish line that separated the living from the dead. My sister and I had prepared to stay overnight with her in her room, but the harsh breathing had made it impossible to sleep, read, or think. I had gone to another small lounge to rest but had soon been called back to the room just as my mother was taking in her final slow, heaving breaths. There had been a pause, then another deep intake of breath. When the breathing stopped, I had waited for another one, even several minutes later, sure it could not yet be the end. So quickly her body altered, emptied of that taut life force that had been our mother, becoming an empty container of flesh and bone and stilled blood.

The time before she died had been infinitely precious, even though she had been mostly unconscious from the time of her admittance to the hospital two weeks earlier after a bad fall and stroke. My sister, my brother and his wife, and I said a few words of prayer together for her, touching a hand, shoulder, leg, or arm, whatever was near. Although I'd left the church as a teenager, critical of the institution's hypocrisy and intolerance and skeptical about its lack of answers to my probing questions, I found no harm in wanting to address my mother's spirit and whatever deity might exist. To our astonishment, our mother suddenly opened her eyes and looked at us for several long minutes. It wasn't a blank flickering or stare, but a fully conscious gaze full of meaning and expression. We murmured to her, "It's okay Mom," "We're all here," "We love you." Her eyes brimmed with tears. Although she could not speak, she seemed to want to communicate something vital to us. It was as if she were aboard a departing train, not wishing to leave. This final gaze was her true goodbye to us—a gift of momentary consciousness.

During those last weeks, I brought my son to the hospital's palliative care ward as often as I could after school. She was his last living grandparent, the last thread linking his generation to hers. Even if my mother couldn't interact with him, they could at least have time in each other's presence. One evening, we even brought a birthday cake to the room so our family could celebrate his birthday together on the day of his birth. After I lit the birthday cake candles in her room, we sang a quick "Happy Birthday." My son quickly blew them out before the nurse came past. "No candles allowed!" she warned us, sniffing the air suspiciously, fortunately too late. During evening visits, he would enter her room briefly to say hello to my mother, sit for a while, and then go to the nearby family lounge around the corner to play checkers with my brother, read, or watch television. At the end of the visits, he would come back to my mother's room to pat her arm or give her a kiss.

"Why is she always asleep?" he asked in frustration.

"When you're unconscious, it might seem like you're sleeping. But sometimes a part of you might be a little bit awake for a few moments even with your eyes closed so you still might be able to hear or feel something," I tried to explain. He didn't seem convinced but continued to follow our lead.

Sometimes I'd pin my son's latest artwork on the bulletin board near her bed. He was especially proud of his chalk drawing on black paper of a rocket zooming past planets and stars. It somehow seemed appropriate. We had all commenced a journey into the unfamiliar. Entering my mother's room in the evenings, I'd see it and ponder the unknown places her spirit would travel to after death. On Chinese New Year's Eve, my siblings and I arranged for our family to have a takeout feast in the hospital with our favourite dishes from the local Chinese eatery we'd frequented while growing up, followed by a sing-a-long in my mother's room. It would be our last family celebration together.

The morning after my mother died, I came to my son's room and sat beside him on the bed. "*Poh poh* died last night," I said, after telling him that I'd received a call to come to the hospital late at night while he was asleep.

He gasped, then burst into tears. "Why didn't you tell me? Why didn't you bring me?" he sobbed. "I wanted to say goodbye!"

I was moved that he felt so strongly about my mother and surprised he seemed unafraid of death. I thought I'd prepared him for her passing, but I wondered now if I should have been even more explicit. I'd worked hard to try to establish a bond between my mother and son from his infancy onward, knowing that the window of opportunity would rapidly close as her dementia advanced. I also knew how much having a grandchild would have meant to her, given her love of babies and children. During the early years, I'd organized weekly family potluck dinners or visits for tea and cake in my home so we could spend time together. My mother had at least been able to hold him for a short while. "Is your baby a boy or girl?" she would ask each time in Cantonese, her ability to absorb new information so damaged that she was never able to recall or even utter his or my name. Most of the time, I wasn't sure if she knew I was her daughter. Occasionally we could coax her to play simple piano pieces for him to dance or clap to. When her condition deteriorated, we'd visit my mother at the secured Alzheimer's floor in her seniors' residence. When my mother was in a good mood, she would ask my son's name again and ask me about my other (nonexistent) children. She'd sometimes try to play or interact with him in small, brief ways, although could become quite anxious when he was out of sight. "Has he been kidnapped?" she'd once asked me when he had hidden around a corner.

Sometimes she could utter a few phrases in English, but increasingly it became mixed up with Cantonese. The words grew more garbled and confused, mirroring what must have been happening inside her brain as dendrites became tangled and neurons withered. Increasingly, my mother's moods grew murkier. She'd often be frowning, unable to make eye contact. She would lunge when my son made sudden movements, as if to grab or even strike him, frightening him and us. When visiting her became more difficult, I would instead show him videos and photos at home of their earlier interactions to reinforce his place in her life and her place in his, remark on their common love for desserts, tell him funny stories from her past and recent past—how as a child she hid behind the stage curtain when performing on the piano for her school, or how as a seventy-four-year-old she would hoard candies around her home. Sometimes it felt as if I were desperately scraping together a relationship out of remnants, shards, and shreds—a kind of mixed media patchwork tapestry riddled with gaping holes, never a whole cloth. But somehow, magically, my son accepted what was so carefully woven for him, without question, flawed as it was. Over those few fleeting years, he came to love his grandmother unequivocally.

As I cradled my weeping son in my arms after telling him of his grandmother's death, I tried to explain to him that I had been worried about waking him in case we'd have to be up all night at the hospital, and about frightening, even traumatizing him. But my apologies, justifications, and platitudes did nothing to quell his despair. He'd wanted and needed to be there. I'd let my uncertainty make me overprotective when I should have given him the choice to decide for himself. It was my fault that his final chance to say farewell to his last remaining grandparent before her death was forever lost. Weeks afterward, he would reproach me for having left him behind.

II

My own response to my father's death from cancer three decades before had been starkly different. My siblings and I hadn't been informed about his prognosis or his final coma. One day after school, my sister and I had come home to a strangely subdued house. Our mother had led us to her room, held us close, and said, "You're father died in the hospital this morning." I had gone completely blank, my body rigid and numb as if trying to reject what I'd just heard, while my little sister had cried in my mother's arms. I had tried to will myself to cry too but couldn't, and never did, even at the funeral and burial. I'd remained in a state of anaesthetized grief for many years, a strangely detached but omnipresent festering ache, as if an invisible limb had been torn from my body that no one could see. Yet here was my son feeling and expressing profound loss openly at age six.

Because of how excluded I had felt from our father's death from cancer when I was eleven years old, I knew how significant that time with my mother before her death would be not only for my son, but for me as well. At the palliative care ward, I talked to my mother, listened to music with her, sang to her, held her hand, stroked her hair. I was finally the daughter I should have been and had wanted to be. It would be the closest I'd ever be to her.

While I was growing up, there had been frequent discord and tension between my parents until my father's diagnosis. After his death, my mother had been overwhelmed with money worries and returning to the practice of medicine. Her towering rages had me fleeing to the basement or my closet. I'd had to hold myself aloof from her to survive emotionally. But much of my childhood anger and hurt toward my volatile mother melted away as I witnessed her gradual mental and psychological decline over a ten-year period. Fissures became chasms as huge chunks of memory fell away, never to be retrieved. Even after her diagnosis, I could not believe the intense, artistic, moody physician mother I'd known all my life was not buried somewhere within her. One time, soon after her initial diagnosis, my brother brought her to my new apartment for a short visit. Uneasy in unfamiliar places, she looked around briefly and then wanted to leave. As I'd been feeling ill all day, I took her hand and placed it on my forehead as she walked past.

"Do you think I have a fever?" I asked plaintively, the way I'd done when I was a child, as if somehow the trained physician in her would break through the fog.

She withdrew her hand quickly and shrugged her shoulders. "Go home now," she muttered to my brother in Cantonese.

The depth of both her memory loss and our loss of our only surviving parent suddenly became clear to me. Not only had all her years of training and working as an obstetrician disappeared, but the last vestiges of her role as our mother had evaporated as well. For weeks I laughed ruefully at my not-so-submerged need to be nurtured. Our time to be cared for had ended long ago. It was our turn to take care of her. My siblings and I were truly orphaned now, even with our mother still alive.

Ironically, I had never needed her more. A few years after her diagnosis, I became pregnant. My relationship with the father was unlikely to endure. I was terrified. In my second trimester, I had a vivid nightmare about being pregnant and somehow accidentally pulling out the three fetuses growing in my womb before they were ready to be birthed. Horrified and panicking at what I had done, I ran to the kitchen sink, filling buckets with water to immerse them, not knowing what else to do. Three translucent-skinned babies floated untethered, oversized heads tucked, little limbs still curled up against their undeveloped torsos. Torn umbilical cords dangling from my body, I ran in my dream to my mother's bedroom, crying out to her to help me save the slowly asphyxiating babies. I was desperate to do anything to keep them alive, to somehow reinsert them in my womb. When I arrived panting and crying at her bedside, I found my mother inert in her darkened room, curtains drawn, just the way she had often been after a particularly long day at her medical practice while I was growing up. "Too difficult," my mother pronounced in the dream, turning away from me.

The next morning, I woke up with an overwhelming sense of dread and futility. My mother could no longer help me—I'd have to face motherhood alone. But there was an additional interpretation. My two siblings and I were shrivelling away in our mother's memory. She would soon cease to be able to recall our names or recognize us—for her it would soon seem as if we had never been born.

When my labour actually began, I was curled by the fireplace alone, feeling vulnerable and anxious. I had arisen to greet my child's father upon hearing his key in the front door lock, when my water broke. On the third day of labour, my cervix had refused to dilate through the afternoon until his arrival at the hospital. The relief and love at seeing him somehow kick-started the contractions, the same mix of relief and love that had led to the start of my labour. After our son's birth, he came to my darkened room in the late evening when the ward was quiet. He held the baby close for a long while. We said little, the silence laden with the unspoken. Even though I knew that our relationship would end, there was a part of me that deeply needed his presence and involvement—his acknowledgment of the significance of the arrival of our child.

A few years after his father moved out, our son and I also relocated to another neighbourhood. We moved into a creaky brown stucco house that at first seemed way too big for us. For six interminable months our son pined for our cozy former abode. "I miss the green house," he'd wail inconsolably, sitting on the stairs with his head in his hands. I felt the same way—he and I had memories of the three of us spending time together in a way we would never be doing again. I remained in a limbo state, still in love with a man who did not love me, hoping in vain that circumstances would change. After my son's father finally told me there was no possibility of salvaging our relationship, I lost a best friend and a lover. The tenuous, imaginary buffer from the realities of single parent-hood that I'd clung to was gone. Those were hard years of overlapping losses: my mother's cognitive and mental decline leading to her death, the departure of my son's father, the end of my child-bearing years, the loss of an opportunity to have a "whole" family.

That winter after my son's father found a new partner, I tried to compensate for those losses by making Christmas extra special—a bigger tree, more decorations, more presents, my first attempt at a homemade gingerbread house. I lugged home the organic ingredients on foot in the rain, carefully followed the multi-day recipe step by step, made the dough, rolled out and cut the pieces, baked them, assembled them. But every step had its tiny crisis. A forgotten ingredient. Extra trips to the store. Shrunken gingerbread segments that wouldn't fit together. Royal icing that wouldn't set. A clogged pastry tube nozzle. Kitchen floor and counters strewn with flour, broken candies, and crumbs. I was covered in flour, then dough, then crumbs, then icing sugar, then icing itself. Finally, one of the two roof pieces broke in half when I was struggling to place it atop the walls. As I grew more frazzled, my son grew more impatient—for him the whole point, of course, was decorating the house with candies.

As I barked, "You'll just have to wait!" to my whining son while I tried to stop the caved-in roof from sliding down with one hand and squeeze more royal icing into the yawning gaps with the other, the self-mocking poet in me was jolted into an epiphany. The metaphorical underpinnings of the whole process became patently obvious. I was trying way too hard to make a home for my son. All my efforts were ultimately irrelevant. Home was neither the building we inhabited nor a decorative seasonal baked good that would be tossed in the garbage in a week's time.

The next year we made a less ambitious, if lopsided house—baking an extra roof piece as insurance after the previous year's debacle. When I burned the gingerbread parents, I just cut out new ones from the extra roof. But I wondered where to place them. The mother and child figures were holding hands by the open front door. "Where should I put the dad?" I asked my son. He shrugged, indifferent. I hovered with the piece for a while, then decided to place the father by the door with his hand touching his son's head so there would be a visible bond between them. As I looked down, it seemed apt—the mother and father were separate from each other, yet joined by their child. I cemented them all down, wondering how long it would last.

III

At my mother's memorial service, my sister and I screened a slide show. We ended it with film footage of our parents' wedding. Our white-satin-garbed mother beamed from the screen as she joined our father in a chauffeured Rolls-Royce idling outside the church, to head off down a Glasgow road into the distance. The man she'd railed against for decades but had deeply loved and grieved for the remainder of her years was awaiting her, handsome and elegant in his morning suit, to whisk her away into the unknown. They were together at last.

My son's father attended the memorial service, sitting in the front pew with my family, minding our son when I had to give my speech and later in the reception hall when I was receiving condolences. Even though he had a new partner and had only met my mother a few times when she had already entered the later stages of dementia, he somehow understood the significance of his presence to both me and our son.

What I fashioned with all the gaps and tears was something new, albeit initially with puckered seams. I would think of C.K. Williams's famous poem, "Invisible Mending," with its description of three elderly seamstresses repairing worn garments:

> how really very gently they'd take
> the fabric to its last, with what
> solicitude gather up worn edges
> to be bound, with what severe
> but kind detachment wield
> their amputating shears:
> forgiveness, and repair.†

Over those years, I had to learn to release past grudges and hurts, and renew or reinforce existing bonds as well as create new ones. With the birth of my son, my brother became a devoted uncle and my sister a doting aunt who would provide invaluable day-to-day support. Because of our mother's dementia, my siblings and I became closer as we worked together to coordinate her doctors' visits, relocation, and care. My mother's illness transformed my relationship with her so that the love and tenderness that had so long been submerged could resurface. Her final stroke and coma allowed me at last to take those necessary steps to forgive both her and myself. Despite the heartache, I did all I could to foster my son's relationship with his father, who remained a stable and loving presence in his life. His father would be there during birthday parties, school plays, and recitals. He would later take our son to Cub Scouts, soccer and baseball practices. And over the course of the years, those puckered seams that had their origins in loss became almost seamless, as natural as if they'd always been there.

A few months after my mother's death, I met a writer friend for our weekly get-together to write. As I started writing, a flood of characters, dialogue, and scenes suddenly broke through the dam of writer's block, spurred by the memory of my son's reproach to me about his exclusion from my mother's deathbed that night, and inspired by his chalk drawing of a rocket that had been pinned to the bulletin board next to her hospital bed. Four barely legible pages later, I had the outline of my first children's book.

I hadn't possessed the power to halt or delay my mother's Alzheimer's, and I hadn't had the chance to have a child until later in my life—but through the alchemy of fiction I could create a relationship between a grandmother and a grandson that could bridge the gap between them and heal the rift that I had inadvertently caused. Here was the grandmother I had tried so hard to show my son, and the grandmother that I knew my mother would have wanted to be. The scenes created themselves: A grandmother spending afternoons making art with her grandson. An exchange of gifts and memories. A shared experience of beauty. The celebration and adaptation of cultural rituals about connection and care after death. A legacy of art and love that would endure.

When I picked up my son from kindergarten later that afternoon, he showed me what he'd drawn that day—a multicoloured striped rocket ascending past a background of stars and planets. It was a startling coincidence that I took as a sign to continue working on the piece. When the story was ready, I read it to him. He listened intently and deeply, as if I'd finally given him the answer he'd needed to hear. I revised the story several more times, and after months of edits, sent out *The Rainbow Rocket*. The story was eventually accepted for publication and endorsed by the Alzheimer Society of BC. Out of my son's despair over the loss of his grandmother came a glimpse of how the heart and the imagination may work together to transform and transcend death, a gift not only to him and to me, but to other children, and to the grieving child that may still exist within any of us.

FIONA TINWEI LAM's first book of poetry, *Intimate Distances*, was a finalist for the City of Vancouver Book Award. She co-edited the literary non-fiction anthology *Double Lives: Writing and Motherhood* (McGill-Queen's University Press, 2008), and also edited *The Bright Well: Contemporary Canadian Poems About Facing Cancer* (Leaf Press, 2011). Her second book of poetry, *Enter the Chrysanthemum*, came out in 2009. Her work was selected for *The Best Canadian Poetry in English 2010* (Tightrope Books). She is a regular contributor to BC's online news magazine *The Tyee*, and her fiction, non-fiction, and poetry appear in over twenty anthologies. Her children's book, *The Rainbow Rocket* (Oolichan Books), was released in 2013. Visit fionalam.net.

†Excerpt from "Invisible Mending," from *Repair* (1999) by C.K. Williams. Reprinted by permission of Farrar, Straus and Giroux, LLC.

Thresholds

LORRI NEILSEN GLENN

1.

Somewhere on the prairie, he has woken to the light on the horizon, checked the bag we bought for his trip—tickets, passport, gum for his woolly mouth. The train is rocking him toward the mountains and we wait at the edge of the country, in the house overlooking the Atlantic where he was raised. We can see the cove, the beach where he and his friends learned to swim. At the front of the house, the deck is cracked from skateboarding crashes. By the driveway, a forsythia bush blooms over the grave he had dug the previous spring for our dog. Inside, the basement room is empty. Upstairs, we move through the days, beginning our own journey, waiting for a clear voice to cut through the dark roar of films that reel behind our eyes.

2.

He was born at night, as so many are. I heard the doctor mention forceps, and I pushed. A strong and robust infant, he thrived on my breast milk and squirmed out of his parents' arms at every turn. Sometimes it felt as though our love was radioactive. Soon after learning to walk, he pushed a chair, unlocked the door, ran naked down the street wearing only a Superman cape. The milkman brought him back several days in a row. We let him crawl under stalls, walk on raised walls, put things in his mouth. He tried everything. Once he bit me, and I bit him back. We never spanked him. He resisted time-outs. If he was going to his room, it was going to be on his terms.

In high school, he grew his hair to his shoulders, gained fifty pounds, joined the drama club, and ate only pizza. He took over the basement room, a place where forks and plates went to die and mould began to thrive. He and a friend filmed their version of *Pulp Fiction: High School* and wrote comedy sketches. He scattered his imaginative drawings on the floor. Once a chatty and articulate child, he now spoke little. His teachers all sang the same song: *if he would just finish . . . if he would just apply.* We faced typical adolescent resistance: it took him weeks to paint the outside window trim. He hit practice golf balls down the hill into the yard of the self-righteous neighbour below us. We urged him to stop (secretly, I was amused), but he didn't.

He and his father bared teeth like dogs; once he slammed the basement door so hard the hinges broke. The fury between them escalated. One morning, in a rare moment of talkativeness, he asked: "If you wanted to dry something slowly, like herbs, how would you do it?" I answered without thinking: "I'd lay it out on tin foil on a cookie sheet and put it on low heat." Later, when the penny dropped, I remembered my own youth when I, too, was blind to others' awareness. The next day I told him to put it all in the wood stove.

3.

The day came: "You have to go," we said. Resistance and anger permeated the house. The kitchen had become a war zone; his little brother, who has an intellectual disability, needed our attention and a stable climate. I became ill. I devoted my time to our youngest, talked with no one, stayed mum with shame. What do you say at a social gathering? Friends wrote holiday letters about their children's law and medical school acceptances, their social justice or volunteer work, their sailing trophies and piano recitals. What could I have written? *Our young son is full of anxiety. Our eldest's eyes are glazed, and last month, he pushed me—once is too much.* Even now, as I write this, I am conflicted. This time it's not about the keeping-up-with-the-Joneses form of motherly shame. It's about ethics, about privacy. Yes, this is my version. Yes, as a poet and essayist, I write to understand. But at what point does my search for meaning run headlong into dangerous waters? Am I violating my son's privacy in writing this?

That day in the kitchen:

"If you don't go, I will. I'll take your brother, leave you and your father to battle it out."

"You grew up in the sixties. Don't tell me you never smoked weed. And besides, both of you drink alcohol, so you have no moral authority."

He moved to the cabin for a few months, kept forgetting to pay rent, or we kept forgetting to ask. When I drove out one morning, I found my grandmother's bone-handled knives, blackened; someone had been freebasing. We thought it was a break-in and had called the police.

We insisted on family counselling. My husband opened up old struggles with his own father; I rethought my reactions to my mother. Our son agreed to personal counselling but went to only one session. My husband and I were confused and felt helpless: What had we done? What could open him up? Where was the sparkplug of a boy we once knew?

The next year our son moved to the city, enrolled in arts, spent his days in a cramped house by the bridge, smoking dope for days on end. He failed the year and lost his financial assistance. He started a series of low-paying part-time jobs, was always short of money. Whenever he visited, we'd check afterwards to see what was missing from the house.

Soon he was on a train headed west and we exhaled for the first time in years. Relieved but terrified, we feared a midnight phone call, a stranger talking of him in the past tense.

4.

Months went by. A year. Another year. Little word. We knew he was in the Canmore/Banff area, moving from one McJob to another. In one of the dozen places he lived, he paid rent to sleep in a broom closet with a folding door. On someone else's apartment floor, he was boot-kicked in the ribs by someone he claimed was a dealer who had the wrong guy.

The phone call came. Canmore detachment. A café, missing funds, a compassionate owner: restorative justice. No record.

We paid to fly him back to the Maritimes at Christmas. My body thrummed with shock: his eyes were like a wombat's; he was rail-thin. He spent most of his visit e-mailing a girl from the rave scene in Canmore. I saw one of the messages when he abandoned the screen. It was full of loathing about his family—our boring life, our too-earnest attempts to talk, our too-curious natures. My gut was on fire; I was beyond tears.

My high school friend, now living in Calgary, offered to rent him an extra basement room with another Maritimer he knew. He wowed them with his inventive cooking and his gardening skills. Soon, however, there were reports of too many late nights, strange odours, broken locks, broken promises. My guilt was piqued when the Maritime roommate phoned me to chide us about our parenting skills. How could she have known we had spent the last several years wrestling with what we saw as our failure, our daily fears for his safety and his future?

I sent his birthday cheque from his grandmother to my friend's address in Calgary, not knowing my friend had already evicted him. Later that week, her basement was broken into. My friend didn't press charges. To this day, he insists he wasn't responsible, but he paid for the window repair, for bars to be installed. And to this day, when I can't find something in the house, my gut lurches, and the feeling is like filthy cold water overtaking my bloodstream. It takes me a few moments to bring myself back to the present.

5.

It's been ten years since he returned to Nova Scotia. He took up DJ-ing, finished a degree in cultural studies, enrolled in a graduate program. He smokes dope rarely, sometimes has a few too many drinks, but it's typical behaviour among his friends. We don't—and can't—say anything. He holds down a steady job, works as a research assistant, has a loving partner, talks of further graduate work. He is eager to help with any task, is thrown into chaos if he senses we are upset. When he is prickly and defensive, I read it as fear of criticism, even when none is intended. (Yet when he reads my writing on our lost years, he has never disagreed, nor repudiated the accounts; he doesn't like to talk about those days). He is often affectionate, even warm at times. The other day he admitted, unbidden, that he wasn't always the hugging kind.

He continues to be wary of tasks he can't perfect. He has difficulty with money, but we don't interfere; they are his priorities, not ours. We are learning—finally—to let go.

His father and I will never know what we did or didn't do, what we should or shouldn't have done. Did we hover too much? Too little? Is our anguish about parenting self-indulgent? After all, children are their own beings. My husband blames himself—his own unresolved problems with his father—more than I blame myself. I love that child deeply and I believe in him; is it naive to think that is enough? Families are complex systems; no one and everyone is responsible.

A friend whose son is an alcoholic said recently: our children can never understand (or even believe) the impact of their behaviour on others. Our son lost years in a fog, time he might have spent developing skills, confidence, focus, the willingness to risk in order to grow. His younger brother is sometimes guarded, has learned not to rely on him, but, like us, is responding to what looks like his older brother's increasing stability. As we have learned to breathe again, we have found other parents—far more than we imagined—with stories that echo ours. All along, we were not alone, but none of us had the courage to talk then. We talk now.

6.

A beloved child gives a couple a foundation, a position from where, as humans, we crane toward a future we'll never fully see. We believed what most parents believe: work hard, be responsible, be yourself. Unconditional love was a credo of our generation; yet some years, the most I could manage was wholehearted. What I did not expect was how our journey would stretch every muscle of the heart, strain it in every possible way, making room for more compassion, more gratitude, more humility. An easy-to-raise child, I realize now, would have made life easier, but not fuller.

And now, we are a family more together than apart. Somehow, I think, our flaws have made us more beloved to each other than before.

Walking on the beach the other day, I found a beautifully smooth stone, almost perfectly oval, but cracked clear through in several places. I could hold it in my hand intact. It had withstood the Atlantic, after all.

7.

Last summer my son and I spent three days alone together, the first time in years, to fix up the cabin to sell. My memory is as vivid as though it were a film.

It's the second morning. He crouches by the front stoop, razor scraper in hand, slicing off the cracked brown paint on the bottom step. His knuckles, gashed from replacing gutter screens in yesterday's heat, are seeping red, and his forearms bear long lashings from the runaway grass trimmer he thought was unplugged.

Weeds, trash, basement room: the first day he had been a welter of energy. By sundown, he was spent. We sat in the porch with glasses of wine, boxes all around, and he held his palms up and out.

"Finally, Mom," he grinned: manly hands. And rolled his eyes. "No one works harder than you," I said.

Today, though, the scraper moves slowly, his hand steady, his gaze focused. This is one of the rare times since he emerged from my body I have seen him still. He looks up when he senses my presence, smiles. "This could take time," he says.

"Well, perfect is the enemy of good," I say. We have a long list, and only three days to finish. He shakes his head. "If a job's worth doing," he starts . . . and begins to hum.

Later that morning, with my head in a cupboard, I pull out a single sock, crumpled bags, a ripped sheet, tubs of cloudy Tupperware, loose pennies. And images that haven't appeared in years. Of a kid kicked in the ribs until he puked blood, a wild-eyed waif in the back of a cruiser in the Rockies, Jim Cuddy in the background crooning "and no one wipes the tears from your eyes." Of that dark Christmas: his restless limbs, gaunt face. Eyes, shades drawn.

After taking out the garbage, I boil water, make the coffee strong and bring two cups to the porch.

The bottom step is now bare wood, stripped of any evidence of paint. A clean slate. His face is calm, open, and his eyes as present as a cloudless sky. He removes the razor from the scraper and replaces it with a fresh one.

"Last step," he says.

LORRI NEILSEN GLENN is the author of several collections of poetry and non-fiction, including *Threading Light* (Hagios Press, 2011) and *Lost Gospels* (Brick Books, 2010). She has edited five anthologies, including *Untying the Apron: Daughters Remember Mothers of the 1950s* (Guernica). Her work has received awards from *Grain*, *Prairie Fire*, *The Malahat Review*, and *CV2*, among other Canadian journals, and has been widely anthologized. Former Halifax Poet Laureate, she teaches poetry, memoir, and creative non-fiction locally, nationally, and internationally.

Going East Through

YVONNE BLOMER

"GOING EAST THROUGH" EXPLORES motherhood through a Japanese form of writing, *haibun*, that interlaces poetry and prose. Matsuo Basho's famous haibun/travel memoir, *The Narrow Road to the Interior*, guided me in some ways. Basho was drawn to the "solitary path of the wanderer" and so this form seemed an apt choice for writing about the sometimes solitary path of motherhood and travel. I have broken many of the rules and I'm not entirely sure how I, or the piece itself, came to this variation from the original form. My hope is that through it a reader can travel west to east across Canada in poems and enter the mother's thoughts through prose so that there is a blending of the two—each leaning toward the other. The poetry leans toward prose and prose toward poetry in the way a mother and child might lean in to read a story, or a husband and wife to hold each other up.

> The Boy looks Captain-like
> in his car seat, gear stacked
> Victoria to coffee at Mill Bay
> home trailing, effervescent
> as the Man accustoms himself to this shadow
> of movement, to this shape. Cobble Hill,
> Duncan, Ladysmith, and stillness;
> the curve of road, of day.

Is it grief or doubt?

She could live a life of unanswered questions. Travelling, they fall away, or are discarded for simpler things—rain, dry clothes, food—concerns that take up the living part of travelling. Sore feet, she finds tiger balm; sun burn, he seeks shade. At the terminal the car disembarks from the ferry and the radio celebrates sound, they watch the road. Driver and passengers alike till the smallest, in the back, sleeps. Think of roadside attractions. Think dinosaurs. Think good coffee and the next potty break.

> #1 East through Vancouver—Chilliwack,
> Hope, to the Coquihalla—
> in the heat of the interior
> sun through the windshield douses
> the Boy's heavy lids in sleep.
> The car hums, awaits
> curve and cloud; Merritt
> to Moon Shadow Campground.

Perhaps both.

Later, in years, the mother will fill like a spring stream and empty. Doubt and grief will be her tide. She does not mean for it to be this way. She does not fully choose it. Worry too. Just before they left, doctors added a diagnosis—ASD.† She'd rather not write about this. She'd rather not be one of those parents. Yet, how else, this story?

> Through sunshine they chase
> storm clouds. Stop for train trestles
> at Myra Canyon, train museum
> at Revelstoke. Thunder and lightning
> overhead, loose rocks
> underneath.

Her son likes to hike. He stomps along in his heavy-footed romp. He goes like this for only a little while, then wants up. Hot. He is hot. But that's not all. That's not it.

Born two weeks early, limp as a levelled boxer, the muscle on his body loose. He likes hiking; he loves the tunnels—cool enough to sit down. He's strong enough now to run. He walked at two years, five months. The mother carries a sarong, she can tie him on; they can go on and on. She'd carry him, she thinks some days, his shoulders getting broader, she'd carry him, she will, for as long as it takes.

> Stop at Rogers Pass—
> travellers—like drops of liquid
> pool in stillness, in the spoon
> of these mountains—look up: sun and cliffs
> and the blue on blue-grey of the Rockies.

The lowly whistle of train as it snakes in and through tunnels. Remember each breath. Birthing him she forced him to come out naturally, worried his lungs would not be developed otherwise. Feeling, in the cells of the tissue that make up the veins around her heart, that this hard work of being born would be good for him. Before she knew anything. Before grief and joy were married. Before he made her the mother she is. Before he was born: quiet whimper, strong breath.

> The Boy's little hand grips their picnic,
> moment apprehended by gleeful squeak,
> while squirrels trail, hopeful,
> he swings snacks perilously from his tight fist,
> eyes back-lit and blue with mischief.

Language is all code. What she grieves are the needs of special. Write these letters on the page: PWS.‡ ASD. Right now—it's all food. While she worries, her son does not. He is in raptures with life. He has his parents to himself. Nothing between him and them but terraced dreams. Nothing but time and the straps of his car seat. He is four. He is, some might say, non-verbal (his mother would not). He is fine, just fine. Rock solid. Rock-hard. Rockies—wahoo—what else is there that is new!?

> At Hoodoo Campground
> the Woman considers—heat, no trees to draw shade,
> bear warnings, and their single car—
> further on at Monarch Campground
> the Man fits their tent in under the trees,
> voices of children playing and
> up the slope behind their sleeping heads
> the Burgess Shale—505 million years—
> trilobites stopped in crush of earth,
> fossils that mark the end of that line;
> and shale, darkening
> under the plum summer rain.

Beware sentimentality.
She reads this in the *Haiku Handbook*. Perhaps she could lean on statistics when she wants to cry/when she begins to cry. On numbers. On things that have already been accomplished. Her son knows his numbers and the alphabet. He signs them, exercising those little fingers into contortions of *W*, *X*, *Y*, and a zippy winged *Z*. Glee in the hand, small those bones, precise and careful they craft letters in air.

> The Man packs up so early the freight trains
> lumber and yawn in the distance.
> Breakfast at Melissa's in Banff,
> then rolling sky, wheat-hued hills,
> the kiss of sun, the whistle of cloud.
> Calgary. The Woman's first Canadian city.

Sometimes her husband disappears from her. Tears when their son was born. The near-retirement Scottish nurse mistook them for grief. Joy, a boy, welled over him. Tidal. Then, he slipped into books he'd already read. She pumped, washed bottles, fought off despair and hysteria—her hormones ebbing, doing their thing. A uterine infection followed by bladder infection—it was a long time between her water breaking and his birth. Maybe a day. Maybe days. Epic and the blink of an eye, that day, those days, that hour. His birth. His time in special care. The time it took her husband to walk the dog. The pumpa-pumpa-pumpa at her breasts and the panic to get back to the hospital until the nurses demanded she rest. Wonder later, now, why she didn't just stay in the hospital.

> Late sleep, lazy day,
> laundry and the Boy
> falls in bass-thrum
> from sofa, to red, to gold, to blue
> cushions thump, thump thump. The slip
> and swish of falling—

Ever have that falling dream?
She has a dream now where he is falling. He slips into water. He runs into their quiet street. He has no concept of danger or his body in space. On the pavement he would not think to watch for cars, to stay on the sidewalk. He'll get this too, though, she hopes. And in water—reckless abandonment—that first pool, his making.

> Laundry now flaps like wings
> fixed to their Pegasus car.
> Magic: the grid of prairie road,
> river and crevasse to Drumheller
> where tuff erodes
> to dinosaur hoof, shank, spine.

Avoiding sentiment is like avoiding the sun.

Her sister quoted to her recently that asking a child with autism to look in your eyes is like asking a blind child to tell you the kind of blue the sky is. Everyone says nothing will change with this new diagnosis, but thinking back, the mother realizes that's not quite true. He's the same child leaving as he was when you came in, says the doctor, who is an expert in such things. Yes, she agrees, he's the same. The filter, though, has changed. Expectation lies to you. But not now, while the sun is trying so hard to stretch her fingers to the earth. Put it on hold another month or two. Drive the miles. Leave the city that is home behind, leave its burdens behind.

> Rorschach of bugs on the windshield,
> of cows in the fields, their black-patched hides.
> The Woman analyzes those shapes, her senses
> thrum.

Anything can be taken away.

What kind of shadow falls on a child's face? She wonders at this question, at those cows. At their mothers. Sadness here, she thinks, calves and their mothers. They had so much to learn after his birth. The nurses in special care didn't think they should spend so much time there. It ached in the groin. It ached in the uterus. It ached in the breasts, so painfully full with milk she had to pump to feed him. Why would anyone want to make someone fight to see their child? They had so much to learn. She pumped for ten months so that he had pure breast milk. What more could she do? He could not feed. With the bottle he did best with his dad.

> At Tyrell the sun hangs like time,
> stalled, boldly, overhead.
> Could the Man and the Boy shimmy up to

that albertosaurus, that triceratops?
Painted purple and orange,
they are hitchhikers,
thumbing their painted toes for a ride;
Prehistoric bleached-blondes,
uncapped, red-lipped,
in the sun they wait to be photographed.

Syndrome: several recognizable features, signs, symptoms, or characteristics
that often occur together. Motherhood, Prader Willi, love.
When friends came to visit, she'd cheer them up. Her answer to that—
her son. So amazing. A small life. Gorgeous. Already flawed, but he
didn't care. In his sleeping loose body, perfection. She'd put a warm
hand on him. Read to him from her first book of poems, the book delivered just days before his birth. Most other babies in the ward were
tiny—preemies—big-footed tadpoles. Her son's hands and feet were
tiny. Like a doll—proportionate for now rather than for what he'd grow
into. This too, part of the syndrome.

But inside—evolution wavers,
a kind of skepticism
nurtured on tales of "Lucy"
but of the reptile variety. Whatever moment—
doubt stunted by hands-on chaos:
children send balls floating on air,
adults rub and sift through memory: shard
of tea cup, shattered bones
in the garden where they dug
the new flower bed.

What is evolution?
Does it have something to do with learning as you go or running to

catch up? The dinosaurs, she sees them with her own eyes, and they are unbelievable. Soy, she said to the neonatologist. Tofu, she said. Nothing you did, the doctor said. But how can that be? In the air that fills her lungs, in the bones that brace those organs, there is a call to action. She would get the yoga pants on, she would get in the car, swallow the lump in her throat, park the car, climb the steps and with him on her belly lie, each week of his first year, in corpse position. The teacher would say: Imagine your mother and your mother's mother, and all the generations of mothers who have come before you. Imagine their experiences as your experiences. Let them hold you up. She would fall through the floor of grief again. Each week she would want to find those mothers there. If they are there, would they catch her?

How to say love in terms of evolution?
How to say error or hiccup—
things get missed. Sometimes arms
fail to form in the womb, or ears,
though the hearing is good.
In the Boy, some small twig,
off some small branch of DNA
deleted in the body's automatic cycle
of creation and correction.

When they are at a party for a friend's kids, she has to be careful about the food. Her son could, if she let it just happen, eat everything in sight. She's never tested it, but it could happen. No one can really believe it. One friend has a son with Down's. The friend struggles to get her son to eat. The friend is in love with her son's appetite. This evolution or genetic blip, too, is hard to believe. Why did some dinosaurs have such short arms? Why in that minute deletion in her son's body did the ability to feel full get lost? How did those strange creatures become birds?

Evidence in gesture over words.
Evidence in smallness of hands and feet.
Evidence in unsated hunger.
Something of the dinosaur, then, in the Woman.
Evidence in his grinding of teeth.
So, stop for a while, get out of the car.

Pledge love again. There are weeks ahead of them. They are so relaxed, laughing up there in the front seat as if and because life is great. Look at them. This is the kind of T-shirt carefree wears. This is the way light-hearted wears her hair, tied back because who wants to bother with it. That giggle from the back seat—that is happy-go-lucky having the day of his life.

The days slow to the shape of weeks,
shape of hoodoos and badlands too.
Through Patricia, along CFB Suffield, to Ralston,
to Suffield, through Redcliff,
Medicine Hat for lunch.
Simon and Garfunkel's "Homeward Bound" on
    the radio.
In Maple Creek, Saskatchewan
they go for a wander, stop for coffee.
The Boy reckless in his teetering,
buoyant, loose limbs.

What did she want out of life?
Not really contentment, though in moments that comes unfettered. Why wouldn't it? How the marrow in her bones craves this boy. How he is getting bigger and bigger and someday she won't be able to swing him up. Someday, he could be stronger than her. Sometimes he finds them in the tent, or in their bed. He crawls in and limpets himself to

her. She can barely breathe; though he's under forty pounds, he likes to hook the top of his head in the crook of her neck. She floats in a state of anchored. In a bliss of being. The questions asked as if she no longer wants anything. What does she want? Life still there in the light of a moment, held.

> They pass Rabbit Blanket Park.
> The Woman thinks — a warm blanket
> (of snow, perhaps) for the rabbit.
> The Man thinks a blanket
> of downy rabbit fur.
> The Boy loves the sound of their voices, rapt.

She had eight litres of amniotic fluid drained by the specialist. He'd draw the long needle in, careful not to pierce what moved inside. Her womb would tremor in that shrinking. Inside out orgasm, hot with pain, her muscles clenching to keep that life in. Twice she had it done. Neither procedure triggered his birth. He held fast, little limpet, in the ebbing tide.

> Rain rabbit blankets the car,
> thick, woolly enough to blind.
> Lake Superior, Old Woman River,
> Michipicoten, all blanketed
> in low cloud, pelts of rain.

Her OB took her off her bicycle. Big belly, granny bike, she had it all sorted. She rode from home to the hospital, then back into town to see her regular doctor. She felt great. Attached to her seat: BABY ON BOARD. She told the OB not to worry about her falling. More likely to fall walking. He stopped talking to her, told her husband to lock up the bike. Her regular doctor said when her heart worked hard it drew blood from the baby's. Lucky to not be put on bedrest. She strolled, dog towing, to the park. Sat on a bench and threw a ball. The dog didn't want to chase, sat, instead, at her feet. Salt. What is sadness? The tears lick at her face.

> The Woman follows big red truck,
> drives, lets him stay close. He passes
> slower traffic, she passes too. Then
> he tucks back behind her.
> Sunlight shimmers
> off red, big red.

Is it enough or too much?
Many marriages end when a child is born with special needs, though she read, early on, they don't have to. This made them both laugh. Some days she thinks her husband is just waiting for the day she's had enough. Every day she's had enough. Every day she can take more. She'd like to fall in love with an older man, a poet. A younger man, no strings. She barely lives in her body. It's all head with her—thinking and thinking and thinking. If only she could anticipate every next corner, prepare her son before it comes. But, maybe she wouldn't. Life to be lived. Chaos too. So, here they are—never still, never moving; always moving, always still.

> In the Woman's lap:
> the map of her country, stretched, thin,
> edged in finger prints, hotel lotions,
> campfire's emboldening smoke.
> The Man drives, listens to "The Hazards of Love,"
> the Boy gazes out the right rear window
> blue of his eyes echoed in everything.

YVONNE BLOMER recently released her second full collection of poetry, *The Book of Places* (Black Moss, 2012), and second chapbook, *Bicycle Brand Journey* (JackPine Press, 2012), which immediately sold out. Her first book, *a broken mirror, fallen leaf*, was shortlisted for the Gerald Lampert Memorial Award in 2007. Her poems have been anthologized and published in journals across Canada and in the US and UK. In 2014 *Caged* will be released by Palimpsest Press.

NOTES
†ASD—Autism Spectrum Disorder
‡PWS—Prader Willi Syndrome. "PWS is a complex genetic disorder that typically causes low muscle tone, short stature, incomplete sexual development, cognitive disability, problem behaviours, and a chronic feeling of hunger that can lead to excessive eating and life-threatening obesity" (British Columbia Prader Willi Syndrome Association, bcpwsa.com).

what you're
not expecting

THE DESIRE
TO UNDERSTAND

A Container of Light

LISA MARTIN-DEMOOR

MOST OF MY LIFE I have been a cynic about the body, its possibility for error, how easily things tip sideways and we are left staring at absence. The year I started kindergarten, I learned how to add and subtract—what happens when you give, when you take away. I grew up marked by the impact of malignant addition, terminal subtraction. Inoperable brain tumours, the piling on of pain in my father's body. Edema that swelled and blurred his face, stiffened his arms. Vomiting that contracted the muscles in his back each time we sat down to eat, drove my sister from the kitchen table. Lumps on his neck and shoulders that bled into shirts my mother washed and washed but could not get clean. When nothing more could be added, my father himself was taken. And so I felt my innocence of the future driven away, because of the knowledge that entered my body.

I grew up cynical, married an optimist. A field biologist who held the legs of songbirds pinched between thumb and fingers and described their plumage to me. We hiked through boreal forest, scrambled above alpine meadows, strolled the banks of the North Saskatchewan River. We walked beneath the ten thousand rustling wings of crows bedding down for the night on electrical wires beside a remnant stand of trees. As we walked, beneath our feet we found the torn feathers of a grouse, the long shadow of a hawk. Death, I saw, is part of the beauty of this world, as painful as it is. And so, I learned to balance here. Walking with my optimist, I found I could stay standing even if the world would not stay still.

But loving an optimist didn't save me. The year Jonathan and I were married, my mom collapsed on the deck of a ferry on her way to Vancouver Island. *Glioblastoma multiforme.* Latin name for a nightmare, two new words for an old story. Three brain tumours—one in the parietal lobe, one in the temporal lobe, and one in the basal ganglia. I arrived a few hours after Mom's surgery, found her in the brain trauma ward of a hospital that sat above the Fraser River, the hospital's architecture and ingenuity opposing themselves to the deep current running through the valley below. I found her resting in bed, her cells enacting their natural right to multiply, divide—but getting the answers critically wrong. She lay propped against the pillows, freckled shoulders draped loosely with a gown, head swaddled in gauze. A hard plastic shunt drained blood and fluid from her skull. I leaned down and put my hands on my knees. But I could not find my balance.

Dying takes a long time, a lot of beauty. I buoyed myself with walks and lilies, laughter and friendship, whatever I could find. Something to place on the other side of the scales that weighed my life, something to shift the balance. Each time I visited Mom and returned home, Jonathan brought me for a walk somewhere—through shortgrass prairie fields east of the city, or along our river which flowed—didn't it, somehow or other—into hers. Once he took me to an old teahouse surrounded by snowy fields, leaned across china cups and farm cream to tuck something into my hands. A tiny silver bird in each upturned palm. Something small and light, a counterweight to sorrow.

When she died, love kept me buoyant for a time, upheld me—though the memory of her broken body, that knowledge, was settling in me. A heavy precipitate, denser than air. And more sorrow was coming, so the wings of tiny birds would not prove strong enough to lift me.

Unbelievably, that year Jonathan's mom found a lump in her breast. Such a small thing, yet with the power of a gravitational pull. *Surely there is a wound at the centre of the world*, I thought.

I can't remember now what happened between us when Sharon was diagnosed—if Jonathan and I wept together, if we walked together, or not. I only remember how exhausted we were by then, going into it. It was not enough—after the surgery and chemo, after she shaved her head and covered it with scarves, after the hair grew in again around her strong and beautiful face, after she had walked alone through the fire and arrived on the other side—not enough that she survived. Survival was not enough to return us to ourselves, to each other—or to return my mother, my father, to me. I remember a slight separation. A loneliness as we watched each other shrink back from our pain, take a last breath and go under, each of us alone in the dark element.

We had not yet learned how much can be survived.

Survival has no resolution, does it? If a threat does not end with its fulfillment, it does not end at all but simply fades. When the time came and we softened toward each other again, it turned out we both wanted the same thing: we were pregnant easily and quickly. We began to look forward together to the probable future. I allowed my heart to explore the possibility of survival. Jonathan's closest sister in age was pregnant too—due three weeks before us—so joy surrounded us, blooming where the threat seemed to have died out.

When I was well into my second trimester and past fear of miscarriage, my twin sister came from BC for a visit. We talked about Mom, who we missed always. I wanted Colleen to hear the baby's heartbeat, which Jonathan and I had first heard four weeks before, and which sounded to me like a spring that bubbles from the ground, becomes a river. The sound had caused me to laugh and cry with delight because I did not wholly believe life could take root in me. Our doctor had to ask me to be still so she could count how many times per minute the tiny heart applied itself to its work, this world. I told Colleen the heartbeat sounded like nothing she'd ever heard: I wanted her to hear the joy I had found where I thought there was a wound.

She never did hear it. My doctor tried a long time to find the heartbeat, then booked me in for an emergency ultrasound the following morning.

℘ To wait for news of the body requires the most difficult form of patience we can be forced into, and causes a physical strain in the heart, the kind of cramp that attends extreme muscular effort in the absence of sufficient respiration.

We had planned to go to the art gallery that night. Once while Mom was still alive, I had tried to take myself to a gallery in the morning before visiting her in the hospital. I knew going to the gallery would keep me bolstered, lifted above the pain that threatened to swamp me. I stood on the wide platform between westbound and eastbound trains and waited for the doors to open — but when they did, I could do nothing but wait for them to close again, then turn away. I saw, suddenly, what was required of me in that moment: to go, to be with Mom in her pain, without being lifted above it. I saw that her pain compelled me to sit with her, to hold vigil, to sacrifice even my own ability to cope in order to stay with — to not escape — her pain. Because she could not escape it, could she? And I needed to get as close as I could to understanding that.

After she died, I started looking for ways to bolster myself again, ways to catch that train. But I found even when I stood before beauty, it no longer had the power to save me. Somehow I had slipped beyond its grasp. The night before my ultrasound I stood in dire need of rescue, on the top floor of the local art gallery, desperate for the skilled hands of strangers to lift me above sorrow. Two artists had painted wide landscapes of mountains, ragged surfaces of rock lit by the bright palette of a setting sun. I tried to pull the paintings into my body, as if they were a force that could displace the knowledge I didn't want. Outside, lights strung through the trees of city hall shone through the windows, and I saw the paintings reflected among the lights.

In the glass, I could see both what was outside the gallery and what was within. Myself and the lights and the paintings, everything contained in a single surface, without separation. I could still feel the baby inside me. My uterus had swelled to the point that I sometimes held the bottom of my belly as I stood up or sat down. In the darkness beneath me, beneath the lights of those trees, I knew more people were suffering, and beyond them, more still — many more than me. And there, in the gallery — I do not remember the artists' names, but I thank them — were the bold brushstrokes of other mortals, praising the fraught beauty of this world. And for a moment I did not feel the need to protect my body, my heart, from what was coming. I saw the lights of the trees, the paintings of mountains, and the curve of my own body in the glass. I saw that the single surface of the world had always included me, and much more than me — and then the feeling passed. So I was left with the superimposition of fear and hope without distance in my heart, which is called courage.

And the balance of the thing determined itself in me.

The baby wasn't alive anymore. We saw an image of it on the ultrasound monitor the following morning, curled on its side. It looked like something settled to the bottom of a pool. What we saw was not the baby, nor its death, but a report of these things, an image carried by sound out of a dark place. I was told I could wait for my body to understand and let go, though no one knew how long this might take. I wondered how deeply my body might refuse to know what it knew. My other option was to check myself into a hospital to be induced. I chose the latter.

They squirreled me away somewhere far from labour and delivery, in a post-operative ward. The on-call obstetrician had left standing orders for every form of morphine, but I wanted to feel what was happening in my body. Physical pain, like a poultice, has a way of drawing out what is hidden in the heart. So I lay in the strange room and cried out the pain of every hospital bed I had ever known—from the first one, beside which my father let me eat the green Jell-O from his tray, to the last one, in which I watched my mother slowly die. I cried out the pain of everything that had been lost in those beds, never to return.

One minute my uterus was soft, a pliant grief, full and empty at the same time. The next minute, a rock revealed itself at the core of me—the hardness of anger, betrayal. Surprisingly low in my pelvis, so at last my body knew, saw the mistake it had made. I understood, then, what had been taken away. My water broke. I had not expected that. I did not know how quickly it would all go, nor did I know how much it would hurt. I watched as my pain became greater than my desire to understand, and I asked for morphine.

At the height of it, I said something to my nurse, and the words broke from me with the force of a physical event. I felt, after speaking them, a surprising desire to push. "I miss Mom," I said, and meant *life is hard, so hard*. The nurse squeezed my hand—bless her—and I pushed then and felt the little thing slide out of me. The nurse called for the obstetrician and there were clamps and little scissors for cutting the cord.

After, the nurse asked if we wanted to see the baby. She brought it to us on a crocheted cloth someone had made by hand. I had not known before that moment that somewhere in my city someone sat making pastel cloths for such a purpose: to palliate the pain of tiny death, wash and clothe its nakedness. The nurse and this crocheting stranger brought us with care toward the thing we needed to let go: she showed us the fingers and toes of the poor, limp, grey thing—the tiny white penis of the boy we had brought this far toward our world, but no farther.

♫ We need to contain light, as well as darkness. So five years after Jonathan's mom had finished her cancer treatments—a major milestone for a breast cancer survivor—and three and a half years after our miscarriage, we flew to Michigan for a family reunion. The reunion had been arranged because Sharon's parents were getting older. It was hard to say how many chances they would have to see all of their children, grandchildren, and great-grandchildren in one place again.

Our daughter Juniper had just turned two years old. One night sitting outside on the deck that overlooked the lake, I saw what I thought was a spark rising from a fire down below. Then another. The sparks faded, but were replaced with more, until the early darkness was filled with fireflies. When we'd boarded the plane earlier in the week, I'd been pregnant again. But sitting in the darkness above the lake, I wasn't pregnant anymore. That day, I'd started bleeding—an early miscarriage, barely a pregnancy at all. Still, a sadness filled me as I watched the fireflies flash from light to darkness and back again—or was it darkness to light and back again? I thought: *either way, it's beauty that allows us to face our darkness*. And I remembered how I used to feel walking with Jonathan, my optimist. The one with whom I'd first learned to balance in this world.

The next evening we took Juniper down by the lake. There was just enough light left for the grass to be brilliantly green, for the fireflies to glow against the deepening sky. They were easy targets, glowing in the grass around our bare ankles, hovering at the backs of our knees.

After the miscarriage it was not hard for us, in the scheme of things, to get pregnant a second time. To have a child at all makes us lucky. But the first year of her life was hard.

It wasn't just the standard sleep-deprivation of early parenthood. The miscarriage had tipped the balance for me. *Not my fucking turn* was what I found myself thinking, back then, losing the baby so soon after losing Mom. I forgot the lights of city hall, and they forgot me. The world no longer felt like a single surface. If I thought of mountains, I thought of the violence of their formation, the thrust and heave of rock as it separated from itself, tore apart. For a time, I let myself weep. Then, almost without realizing it, I began to get angry.

One day, in a banal domestic moment, the anger surfaced. Juniper was about a year old, and I was making a last-minute supper. All that happened was this: in a rush, I lost control of a fried egg, and it sailed across the kitchen table. "Fuck!" I said, waving my egg-flipper in the air as the egg hit the table. Jonathan looked startled, yet tired—accustomed to my irritability, easy frustration. "Fuck!" I said again, lest I be misunderstood. I felt the world was made up of accidents like this one—a dropped egg, a flawed fetus, malignant cells—errors accumulating constantly in the dark, and I was tired of bumping into them: it hurts to stumble around, alone, in darkness.

Then something happened: Juniper looked up, tipped her head to one side, made a face at me, and smiled.

And I thought: *My God, she's trying to make me feel better—my little girl is trying to lift me.*

And there, across the table where my fried egg lay critically wounded, I saw the most basic choice I believe we make in this world: who to blame, who to hold responsible. I saw how the anger that had been flickering beneath the surface of my life, unacknowledged, had been affecting my daughter, my husband, our life. And the single surface of the world cohered again for me, pulled me out of hiding. In the light of my daughter's eyes—which were the same as the lights below city hall, weren't they?—I saw there is a line between pain and culpability.

And I had crossed it, tipped the balance.

I think I got angry because I believed other people's happiness in their good fortune was arrogant, ignorant—even unkind. Now I am learning another way to respond, how to be responsible for my own pain. How to sit through the fire of my anger and let what is not love be consumed. These days I am thinking about joy—the only way I know to edge out anger. Maybe pure, surrendered joy, if it truly honours what we have, can also acknowledge what we lack —the very things we and others suffer for lack of.

And what do we lack? Someone to sit with us in our sorrow, willing not to be lifted above it. It is not only the beauty of the world that saves us. If we let it, something else can save us too —our responsibility for this world, for our pain and each other's.

🖎 When I was three months pregnant with Juniper, I thought I felt her move for the first time. A brief flutter low in my uterus, in the place I had once felt myself turn to stone. Unbelievably, at our next appointment, our doctor could not find a heartbeat. A silent miscarriage —that's what it's called when a baby dies without the body noticing, a loss that goes unheard. Our doctor sent us straight to a nearby hospital, where the radiologist spread cold jelly over my abdomen, prodded me with the ultrasound wand. I turned my face away, and wept.

And then the balance tipped, something was added that we thought had been taken.

"Oh," he said. "There *is* a heartbeat." He smiled and swivelled the screen toward me.

I turned to see the grainy image of our living baby, lines of light defining her from the darkness, tumbling around inside my body.

🖎 All around us, fireflies light up the darkness, then disappear. Things are always being added, taken away. We catch the fireflies in our hands, tuck them into the plastic container. Juniper toddles after us to get a look. Tiny lights blink in and out over the grass and I think of the lights below city hall, the light of Mom's hospital room seen from the river. I want my daughter to build a muscle for this world, learn how to balance here, navigate by its lights and by its darkness.

So many fireflies down by the lake. She wants to hold them all in her container, doesn't want to let any of them go. I prefer them wild, sparks of light that rise and vanish over the grass, each one a surprise that glows only long enough to be noticed, then fades before I have a chance to miss it. But when Juniper loves something, she doesn't wonder how much she should love it, doesn't sense an end coming. She is teaching me innocence—how, right now, to love what I love.

I kneel beside her, my fingers curling around the blue lid, and I try to explain what else I've learned about love, how it survives distance. How light is always leaping out of darkness, even when a light we love goes out. I tell her what we have to do: the container must be opened, the light returned to the world. She is watching every move I make, because I am teaching her how to let something go. And I am watching every move *she* makes, because she is beautiful, and I am responsible for her, and she is teaching me how to open my heart again.

She cries when we set the fireflies free.

LISA MARTIN-DEMOOR lives in Edmonton, a few steps away from the river valley, with her partner and two children. No stranger to writing about loss, she won the 2009 Alberta Literary Award for Poetry for her first collection, *One Crow Sorrow* (Brindle & Glass, 2008). Gaspereau published her long poem "Assertions of Likeness" as a chapbook in 2010. Her work has appeared in a broad range of literary journals in Canada and has been broadcast on US and Canadian radio. "A Container of Light" won *The New Quarterly*'s Edna Staebler Personal Essay Contest and a National Magazine Award for Personal Journalism. Lisa was awarded *The Malahat Review*'s Open Season Award for Poetry in 2013. She is currently at work on a novel and new poems, and keeps a blog about writing and motherhood (among other bright extremities) at writerinresidence.ca.

Opening the Griefcase

MAUREEN SCOTT HARRIS

I'm telling you a
story to let myself
think about it. All

day I've been
here, and yesterday.
The months, years,

enclose me as
this thing with arms
and legs. And if

it *is* time
to talk about it,
who knows better

than I?

—Robert Creeley†

1. COMING TO GRIEF

I don't come to grief in a single step. My trek begins with restlessness, a moody discontent with my life—either it's empty, or it's too full. I never foresee this mood and I don't know how to drive it away. I pace from room to room, hoping for distraction that doesn't come. Slowly I am worn down and sink through restlessness into anxiety. What's *wrong* with me? As if in answer, despair and an aching sadness rise from the soles of my feet and I feel as if I'll dissolve in tears. I resist crying because once started I'll never stop. The resistance settles heavily into my chest, flattening my heart and blocking my throat.

I try to write through my choking heaviness, but after a while my thoughts and arms are so heavy I can't think how to continue. Then restlessness returns to rescue me from the going-nowhere scribbling. I abandon my page and answer a phone call, sort some books, make a grocery list. One day, after a few weeks of this start-and-stop writing, I decide it's useless, the writing amounts to nothing. I allow myself to be reclaimed by the minutiae of daily life, neglected while I huddled in grief's shadows.

2. FULL OF HOLES

When I write I'm turning my life over to language. I want to find the line of continuity between now and then, making a map through time. But again and again I find myself where words fail me and the line is broken, the map left blank. In those places my narrative falters, breaks down. Or up. I'm left with a story—and a map—full of holes.

My grief is such a place, a place where language has failed me. Or I've failed it. Grief presses forward, longing to be put into words—

But the truth is I want to find words and avoid grief. Longing and avoidance push against each other and achieve a stand-off in silence. This part of the story is beyond me. Here everything falls away into the blank space on the map. I'm empty, haunted by my wordlessness. How can I *write* wordlessness, its vertiginous spaciousness?

3. BAD BABY DREAM

I'm somewhere with my parents. We've come back to a house where there's a demanding and unpleasant baby dressed in a brilliant red sleeper. Earlier my father had tried to take his picture, but every time he arranged the child's head at the angle he wanted, the baby pulled away or cried. We go into the house. I see by my father's set face that he's expecting trouble and already annoyed. To forestall his anger I scoop up the child. How tiny and insubstantial he is! Earlier he had so much energy and was so troublesome. Now he is limp with floppy arms and legs like a doll's. The warmth of his little body against my chest sends a wave of tenderness through me. He's quite beautiful, with large dark eyes and a head of dark hair. His face isn't really a baby face. I take him to another room to get away from my father's seething anger. Waking from this dream I'm not sure where I am.

4. OPENING THE GRIEFCASE

When my younger daughter, Katharine, was a toddler, she called my briefcase my griefcase. It seemed so apt I never corrected her. I was always stuffing things into it that gave me grief—half-finished poems, half-written letters, half-read books. The life I longed for and couldn't seem to reach.

When I open the griefcase I find a particular story. It's one I've swallowed, or tried to. If I'm to write it, I must track the story's lost and forgotten details through the broken terrain of emotion and memory, that place I have no map for. Where to begin? Possibly in Saskatoon where, in 1964, I gave birth to a son. I was two weeks past my twenty-first birthday and not married. I can't remember the name of the hospital or the day of the week or whether he was born in daylight or after dark. For many years I couldn't remember the date. I saw the baby three times: once in the delivery room where I had to demand to see him; once in an empty room in the hospital where a nurse unwrapped him so I could see that he had all his limbs and all his toes; and a third time about three weeks later, alone in a room at the courthouse where I had just signed the papers that took him for adoption.

5. IN THE CAR

On June 1, 1964, my mother drove from Winnipeg to Saskatoon to collect me and bring me back home. I remember wanting desperately to be back in my own room in my own house. I was full of feelings I couldn't name then, but recognize now as a rich brew of relief, anger, unhappiness, resentment, grief. I was eager to see her, and also afraid of her justified anger and disappointment. Afraid, too, to see she didn't love me.

When she called to say she was bringing my sister Pat for company on the drive out, I asked if Pat knew about the baby. "No," my mother said. I understood then there was to be no conversation about what had happened.

In the car my mother didn't say a word of anger or disappointment. I stared out the window and said little myself. What was there to say?

6. UNSEEMLY

I understood I had to keep my pregnancy a secret. I'd read enough *True Confessions* (hiding the magazines under my mattress) to know that sex outside of marriage meant you were beyond the pale. It was the early 1960s, and birth control wasn't yet legal. A white wedding was the high point of a girl's life, and I was damaged goods. I was also a minister's daughter and the damage was collateral. For my parents, my pregnancy had been evidence of some profound failure on their part and they were full of their own hurt and bewilderment.

We weren't a family practised in sharing feelings, especially not *bad* feelings like anger or sadness. All extravagant feeling was unseemly, but bad feelings were a kind of dirty secret. Maybe we felt that bad feelings made us bad people, or that we were—or ought to be—above the failings of ordinary people. Believing ourselves exemplary, how could we encompass our fall from grace? Mutual silence was our strategy, a strategy guaranteed to keep us safe and at a distance from each other's hurts.

What would have happened if we *hadn't* kept our feelings distant? If we'd yelled at each other and cried? My mother hated tears. Whenever she cried, which was rarely, she got angry. For most of my life I believed she was angry at me because I'd made her cry. Now I think she was angry at herself.

7. THINNESS

It's six weeks since my baby was born and I'm supposed to be thin, my old self again. I've put on my favourite dress, the one I've dreamed of wearing. But it's a struggle to pull it down over my body and its short sleeves pinch my arms. The rows of vertical pleats on the bodice pull and gape across my post-pregnancy breasts. I'm fat. I look terrible. I storm out of the bathroom and past my mother coming up the stairs. "I'm going for a walk!" I snap at her.

I remember the look of my arms and the despair that washed over me and passing my mother on the stairs. Then I'm walking down my old street on a summer evening, feeling the air cool on my thick arms in their tight sleeves. The late sun halos trees and houses and casts deep shadows, like gaps, across the sidewalk. The leaves on the trees fold sunlight and shadow together. It's hard to see where I'm going.

8. BACKWARDS

I think I must have been born backwards or upside down or folded up, not headlong or feet first, it's taken me so long to try to deliver memory with its thin wail, its newborn feet kicking. And how reluctant I am to hunker down to the work. I've written these few pages and anxiety is thick in my stomach, my arms feel weak. I'm terrified at what I'll find kicking on the table when the work's done. But I mustn't let it go again.

Whether I remember it or not the story lurks and hovers. It's every-where in my life — in my poems of loss and absence, my persistent sense of dislocation, my readiness to feel at fault whatever goes wrong. It's in these boxes of unfinished writing stacked up all over my study. I'm surrounded by clutter because I won't, can't, let anything else go. I'm haunted by irrational fears that are rooted in giving up a child, but that rise like a smokescreen to divert me when I approach the story.

I delivered a child and I gave him away. For years afterwards I felt hollowed out inside. Now I feel stuffed and choked. But maybe that's an illusion, a kind of hysterical pregnancy of the emotions. If I bear this story and give birth to it, as I did the baby, I'm afraid it will evaporate, leaving me empty again.

9. GRATEFUL

In the summer of 1964 my family moved to Toronto and I went with them, transferring to university there. Sometime in September I heard from the Saskatchewan Social Welfare Department that the baby had been adopted and was doing well. During the next two years I finished my degree and won the Governor General's Silver Medal. I travelled briefly, and married. Before our marriage I told my husband about the child I had given up for adoption. We didn't talk about it much. He said it didn't matter and I wasn't going to push my luck. I was grateful to him for being willing to marry a girl like me. Though it wasn't his intention, his silence functioned as an extension of the family silence, reinforcing my feeling that what had happened (what I had done) was unspeakable. I was determined to be a very good wife indeed to make up to him for my unmarried pregnancy. The child didn't come into it.

I became a librarian and seven years after I gave away that child I gave birth to my first daughter, and seven years later my second. Over those years the months in Saskatoon became the past and (as the past is supposed to) receded to the back of my mind. But other things faded, too, principal among them my belief that I might someday be a writer.

I'd started to write in high school and become serious (if uncertain) about it at university. Then came my pregnancy during which I wrote nothing except a journal of sorts and opaque letters home. Back at university I made sporadic attempts at poems, but mostly I recycled pieces from my other life, the one before the baby. I still talked about writing though, and when I met my husband I told him that's what I hoped to do. Throughout the early years of our marriage I kept a little black notebook with me where I jotted down inspired lines or ideas, titles of books, and bits of conversation I overheard. But nothing came of those notes and eventually the notebooks themselves faded from my consciousness.

10. FALLING

Sometimes I used to wonder if I'd made the whole thing up, if none of it had happened. Maybe it was all a bad dream, or some perverted fantasy. If it had *really* happened, wouldn't I know his birth date? What mother forgets her child's birthday?

And what about the child? *My* child. Maybe I'll never know what's become of him. He could be hurt or abandoned. Maybe he hates me. With that thought I start to fall. I can't stop myself. It's the nightmare I can't wake from.

11. FRAGMENTS

For roughly twelve years I didn't write at all. My life was full of house, children, husband, and part-time job. Nothing in it led me to writing. I was so busy that often I could barely scrawl a grocery list.

I was in my early thirties when I began to find slips of paper with words written on them stuck in books, or buried in the unanswered letters and papers on my desk. Not lists, which I made a lot of, but an image or a line of poetry, even once or twice a stanza. I didn't recognize any of them though they were in my handwriting. Slowly I started changing or adding words, then lines. When I had a handful of perhaps-poems I decided, uncharacteristically, to find out if they were real poems. I took them to a writers' workshop.

The instructors took my poems seriously and made suggestions and comments. During the next several years I alternated between writing as steadily as my life allowed, and despondency about my work. Sometimes months went by when I didn't write a word. Occasionally I sent poems out to journals, and occasionally one of them was accepted. Occasionally I began to think I could put a book together.

Finally I had a manuscript of sorts, and a publisher who was interested in helping me develop it. That process too was spread out over years, while I left the editor's comments under my desk, or couldn't bear to look at a particular poem again. Then one day I stood in the kitchen holding the proof of my book in my shaky hands. I cried and cried and cried. I could hardly believe it was real. My book was published in 1993, the year I turned fifty, and fifteen years after the workshop. It was beautiful. I could hardly wait to get to the next one.

12. DROWNING

April 1994. It's almost a year since I held my book in my hands and I'm not writing much. I can't seem to settle enough to write. I've just turned fifty-one —

If *I*'m fifty-one, the child I gave away is about to turn thirty. Thirty. *There is no baby out there, floating somewhere above the surface of the earth, waiting for me to find him.*

My throat constricts, my breasts ache, grief swamps me like illness. No matter what I do now I'll never hold that baby in my arms. Never. I stand in the bedroom holding a book and howling, awash in nausea. I can't pretend any longer that I'm all right. I'm going down for the third time.

13. WRAITH

On May 9, 1964, I wrote in my journal: *I have a baby boy, born last night some time after 9:00. He weighed 7 lb., 8 oz., and looked huge. I haven't really seen him yet. They let me give him a name, which somehow makes him a little more mine than he was. I have called him Sean —*

But I've hardly ever called him Sean in my mind. I've hardly ever called him anything. I've pushed away that glimpse of him in the delivery room and I've never let myself imagine him. Except on those occasions when grief rises and knocks me flat. Then I'm so caught in my own mess of feelings that he remains a wraith, thin as air.

Where that baby was is a void, an empty space—the emptiness inside I felt for years. I'd known him inside my body, but even there I didn't attend to him because my attention was directed toward getting *through* the pregnancy. Because I didn't hold him and look at him, when I try to imagine him I encounter that unmapped blank space into which words won't come and across which I can't travel. I glimpse nothing. If I strain to see, all the feelings I tried to turn my back on well up into the nothingness, more unbearable even than it. My choice is to be empty and silent, or full of an anguish that takes my breath, and voice, away.

14. BESIDE MYSELF

What I can't bear in my pregnancy journal is its opaque emptiness— there's nothing in it but remarks about the weather, lists of errands, and notes from the books I was reading. I feel my throat close as I realize that my life then was so unbearable I never wrote from inside it. And my writing *still* struggles with the same seemingly insurmountable difficulty; again and again it refuses to be *in* my experience. How often I live beside myself!

I see that's how I got through the pregnancy. I treated the days as absolutely normal, getting up, doing whatever I had to do that day, taking my walk, writing letters, unpacking groceries, playing with the kids of the couple who had taken me in, joining the neighbourhood women in their morning coffee and conversations. As if this was just my life, not remarkable, not sad, not lonely, above all not unusual. As if I could be anyone. As if it would go on that way forever.

15. KNITTING

If I'd been able to go on that way forever, I needn't have given birth or given up the son who looked like me. Perhaps that's what I hoped to achieve, to spin out the pregnancy forever. Never to have to lie on my bed in the four-bed ward alone, while other women visited with husbands and parents. Never to sit with the curtains pulled round me hearing the sounds of nursing babies. I held him only once in the confines of that tiny room in the courthouse where I surrendered my legal right to him. I think he wore yellow—knitted sweater and hat. Had I made them for him? I remember knitting a tiny yellow sweater for my friend Lynne whose first baby had just been born.

I can't remember!

And it's not in the journal.

I didn't keep the baby, and I didn't keep the story—I didn't even keep my own experience. Not writing the story reiterates my refusal of my life; it tries instead to keep me safe from it.

16. SNAKEBITE

I dream a snake lunges at me out of a crawlspace beside some deserted basement stairs. I race up the stairs to escape, the snake quick behind me. Just as I near the door out I glance over my shoulder—its bright yellow mouth is wide open and as I watch its blunt orange fangs plunge into my right wrist. I turn my hand, somehow grasp the snake's body, and with all my strength try to crush it. Something cracks, but the snake doesn't let go. My heart pounding, I yank myself awake.

Later I tell this dream to a friend. She looks at me and says, "Is there something in your life you feel you haven't done?"

17. HAIR

I've got to do something but I don't know what. I stare at my face in the mirror as if my reflection might tell me. But my hair gets in the way. I pull it back from my face and then can't bear what I see. It's as if my face belongs to someone I don't want to be. A voice in my head says, *It's time to occupy your face.*

My daughter gives me a buzz cut. Mind roiling, I watch my hair fall. I remember an image, ghostly now, from a black and white movie: a young woman has her head publicly shaved for collaborating with an enemy soldier. She must have had sex with him. I remember the scene as terrifying, the people around her implacable. Marked and identified as a transgressor, she'd never be safe again. I'm not a young girl or woman anymore, but it's years since I've felt safe. I'm still waiting to be found out and punished.

I'm sacrificing my hair and my hiddenness. I take a handful of hair and fling it under the cedar tree by the front porch. I'm offering it *in exchange for my son.* Let me find him alive.

I contact Saskatchewan Social Services and learn they will search for him. It's time to write, too, and I outline an essay about the conjunction of giving up a child and not writing. With it I am accepted into a creative non-fiction workshop in Saskatchewan. As I'm packing to leave for it I hear from a social worker in Regina. She thinks she has located my son. I'm to write him a letter without identifying information. She will then contact him with the letter to see if he'll consider meeting me. She tells me his name is Stuart.

They let me give him a name, which somehow makes him a little more mine than he was. I have called him Sean —

But who is he, this person called Stuart? What does he have to do with me?

18. SECRET

August 7, 1997, St. Michael's Retreat Centre near Lumsden, Saskatchewan. I put the phone back down in its cradle, my sweaty hands shaking, heart in a staccato frenzy. I walk back to my room hoping not to run into anyone and sit down in front of my computer. I'm trembling and can't think. I stare at the screen as if it might flash me a message. It's 4:30 in the afternoon on the final day of the workshop and the call was from the social worker. *Stuart has agreed to meet me, if I can get to Edmonton.*

I don't want to talk to anyone about anything. I go outside and walk through the valley, squinting, light-headed under the summer sun. When I come back in it doesn't occur to me to tell people, not even the people in my writing group who have been helping me sweat my story onto the page.

It's *my* secret. I don't want it taken away from me.

19. HANDS OUT

April 14, 1999. In ten days I'll be fifty-six, which means in twenty-four he'll be thirty-five. It's a year and nine months since we met. I remember him getting out of his shiny red pickup truck, and me walking across a lawn toward him. He put out his hands to me — I wonder if he remembers? — and I couldn't speak. That evening his mother asked me if I would tell him the story of his birth. I couldn't do it then, but months later I wrote him about those moments in the delivery room when I was exultant and demanded to see him. Did I tell him he looked just like me? The delivery room had receded and there we were, just the two of us. I remember my shock of pleasure when I saw a blurry version of myself in his little face! For a moment I felt powerful. Then they whisked him away.

20. HOLDING

The night we met, Stuart cooked dinner for me and his parents, who had driven from Saskatoon to be there. They welcomed me and invited me to visit them on my way back east, to see baby pictures and hear their stories about him. I went and was given glimpses of a dark-eyed, dark-haired toddler and child, a cocky adolescent. Glimpses too of the love and warmth that had surrounded and held him.

Held him as I hadn't. Meeting him, meeting them, seeing those photographs, I began to understand what I'd missed and what I hadn't mourned. I might have imagined a life for him over all these years, allowed hopes and fears for him to grow (as he grew in his life, elsewhere), and so had something for myself, something I could offer to him now: the once-upon-a-time story of a life I'd wished for us. Instead I'm impoverished, with nothing to say.

21. WANTING

I will never see the back of Stuart's baby head, never trace with eye and finger the spiral of his dark hair, the way I traced that pattern on the heads of both my daughters. I'll never watch him build a fort, make snow angels, or draw a house. I'll never teach him the names of birds or show him the flowers growing in ditches as we walk. I think about all the time that's gone, full of a longing so sharp and deep I can hardly catch my breath. I'm sunk in the rich details of the grief I've held off for years. The waves of it rise and crash down on me again and again. I don't run from them. And I don't drown.

22. WRITING-NOT-WRITING

For years I've been writing-not-writing about my pregnancy and the baby I gave up. Time and again I've laboured to make space for writing as if words would just well up and fill the page. But the page stayed blank because what wells up is not writing or words, but feelings, and those I can't bear. Writing inevitably leads to the void in the centre of my life, a void woven of three interlaced absences: the absence of the child, the absence of words for his absence, and above all the absence of the feelings that might generate words.

Writing-not-writing has been my way to keep myself from finishing the story because I don't want to find myself at its end, empty-handed and without the child. *I will never have the life I might have had with that baby and child.* Can I stop clutching at the impossible? What I can and do have is my grief. It tells me that what happened is real, I didn't make it up. Writing down a line of words *can* make a line of continuity between then and now, resurrecting and then stitching in my missing feelings. Then the feeling self is alive and at home in the world, even if grief-stricken.

My grief has been faithful to me for years. It is that thing with arms and legs enclosing me that Creeley writes of. It lies here in the endless drafts for this essay, but it has also leaked into my poems and woven the complex constrictions in my thinking and words. I know it *is* time to talk about it. And to it.

Look, I say to my grief, *at all the ways I have inhabited you. You are the thread that runs through my life, the story I can't help but tell when I open my mouth.*

Poet and essayist MAUREEN SCOTT HARRIS was born in Prince Rupert, grew up in Winnipeg, and lives in Toronto. She has published three collections of poems: *A Possible Landscape* (Brick Books, 1993), *Drowning Lessons* (Pedlar Press, 2004), which won the 2005 Trillium Book Award for Poetry, and *Slow Curve Out* (Pedlar Press, 2012). Harris's essays have won the Prairie Fire Creative Non-Fiction Contest (2006), the Sparrow Prize for Prose (2008), and the WildCare Tasmania Nature Writing Prize (2009).

†"Than I," from *The Collected Poems of Robert Creeley, 1945–1975,* by Robert Creeley, © 2006 by the Regents of the University of California. Published by the University of California Press.

Fall and Spring

KIM AUBREY

KATHRYN'S STUFF FILLS THE back of our Subaru wagon—two camp bags full of jeans, concert T's, and tennis shoes, her laptop and printer, a box of books and CDs, a plastic bag bursting with linens and coat hangers, the electric guitar we bought her one Christmas. Slipping into our usual places in the car—Joseph in the driver's seat, me beside him, Kathryn in back—we begin the half-hour drive from our suburban home to the University of Toronto's downtown campus.

Driving along Mt. Pleasant, I lull myself into thinking that we're only taking her to a dentist appointment, not to live in a university dorm. But as trees and houses give way to apartment buildings and offices, neither Joseph nor I can resist giving anxious, last-minute advice:

"Follow your interests."

"Be sure to get enough sleep."

"Take the vitamins I gave you."

"Have fun, but not too much fun."

"Don't do anything that doesn't feel right."

Kathryn's lips barely hold back a smile as she listens with uncharacteristic patience, knowing that soon she won't have to.

A few blocks from the university, we pass our old brick apartment building on Charles Street.

"That's where we lived when Kristine was a baby," I say, craning my neck to look at the window on the sixteenth floor.

Kathryn follows my gaze. "You say that every time we pass here."

"That window in the corner with the orange curtains."

I'd spent hours staring down at people on the street, or into the windows of the apartments across the way, longing for something other than my own sequestered life with baby and husband.

I almost say, I was your age then, but I don't want our past to intrude on her future any more than it already has.

Soon we're approaching the dorm, a few blocks west on the same street. Fresh-faced students direct traffic, answering our questions about where to park. Six years ago, we helped Kristine set up her room just a few blocks away on the same campus. Now she's starting a PHD in social and political thought at York in the city's northwest.

Kathryn's room is on the second floor, overlooking a playing field behind the stores and apartments of a shopping plaza where, twenty-five years ago, I drank coffee with my best friend, Heather, who was visiting from Bermuda where we both grew up, while Kristine slept in her stroller beside us.

Her roommate hasn't arrived, so Kathryn takes the bed by the window. On the wall over the other bed, a poster promotes safe sex — a black and white photo of a young woman, eyes half closed, lips parted, breasts partly bared. I look away, read a list of rules taped to the desk — no candles or incense, a twenty-dollar charge for lost keys.

Joseph plugs in Kathryn's printer, fiddling with her laptop while she hovers behind him, saying, "I can do that."

"Do you want help making the bed?" I ask.

"I can do it."

"Should we go? Are you sure you don't need help?" My empty hands are tense, fingers curling in as if I might hold onto her a little longer. Six years ago, we'd stayed at least an hour setting up Kristine's computer, helping her find space for her things.

Kathryn bounces on her toes. "I'm going to unpack. You can stay or go."

"We'll leave you to it then," says Joseph.

She walks us to the elevator, which opens to release a young woman with twice as much luggage as Kathryn brought. I remember the trunk my father and Joseph carried up to my dorm room in southern New York State twenty-six years ago, my mother helping me to unpack, stretching familiar sheets from home over the single bed. Sheets that had hung on a clothesline beside a banana tree, a pillowcase that smelled of ocean breezes.

My father had commented on the blank uneven walls, the rusty radiator, the worn floorboards, while I'd admired the big closet, the crown moulding, the bright window overlooking a green campus. But I'd wept after they left. My parents hadn't known that my period was several weeks late, my life already veering away from this place where I'd just arrived and wanted to stay.

Kathryn gazes out the window at the freshly mown playing field.

"Are you sure you have everything you need?" I ask.

She shrugs. I can't read her expression. Is she anxious for us to leave so she can start her new life? Or putting on a brave face, pretending to an independence and maturity she doesn't feel?

No, that was *me* at her age—pregnant and scared. Now, standing here with Kathryn in her dorm, emotions from my own first day of college flood back, filling this room, so that I can't tell who's feeling them—her or me.

The day after my parents and Joseph left me at the dorm, I woke with the sun in my eyes and squinted out the window at students heading off to the cafeteria—girls dressed alike in their brown print granny dresses and clogs. The other freshmen seemed to know their way around already, seemed to be having fun. When my roommate brushed her long, blond hair, pulled on straight-legged jeans, the only fashionable alternative to granny attire, and looked past my bed on her way out the door, I knew we'd never be friends.

We'd been assigned this sunny room because we both came from warm climates, but she was a California girl and I grew up in Bermuda, an island in the middle of an entirely different ocean.

At the college store I shopped for textbooks, tins of orange juice and boxes of crackers. Already I'd begun to feel nauseous in the mornings. My body knew I was pregnant but I tried not to listen. For the sunny window beside my bed I bought a creeping charlie trailing hundreds of small, shiny green leaves.

That night I went to a party in the quad with some girls from my dorm. I didn't stay long, walked back by myself, savouring the nighttime anonymity, watching dorm windows darken on my approach.

The next day I consulted the campus map and made my way to the clinic. I needed to know before classes began. I'd promised Joseph to find out as soon as I could. The probability that I was pregnant had hung over me like a fog obscuring my future. The test would determine the shape of my semester, never mind the shape of my life.

Late June, my parents and brothers had gone to our cottage in New Hampshire for the summer, but I'd insisted on staying home in Bermuda. I'd be going to college soon and wanted to spend all the time I could with Joseph. My parents had agreed, on condition that I lived in my grandmother Lorna's spare bedroom and worked at my father's jewellery store in Hamilton. From the back terrace of Lorna's first-floor apartment, I could see the distant sloping white roof of my own house, "Avalanche," which my parents had rented to tourists for the summer.

One Sunday evening, after Lorna made dinner for Joseph and me, the two of us went out to meet friends. When we returned, Lorna's bedroom door was shut, the TV blaring. Joseph and I crept into my room, closed the door. We'd been having sex for three or four months but I'd only recently begun to reach orgasm. The first time, seeing something like fear in his eyes, I'd worried that I'd lost him. Now I lay on top of him, willing our two bodies to meld together so I'd never have to be alone. When we finally slid apart, I opened my eyes to a strange dark room, which smelled of roses and salt.

Later, I listened to Joseph's moped rev up and rumble away down the hill. I'd be joining my family in New Hampshire soon, then on to college. I felt sad about leaving, anxious about going away to school on my own. Lying in bed, I wrapped my arms around my chest, holding onto opposite shoulders, trying not to cry.

My period was late. We'd used condoms until Joseph read about the rhythm method, but I didn't have as much faith in it as he did.

If I lay still, I could hear the hum of Lorna's television. If I lay very still, I could smell Joseph's salt and pepper scent lingering. I could feel the pulse in my forehead, the swell of my breath, but I couldn't feel the pregnancy taking root in my uterus, couldn't see the future taking shape ahead of me, or remember crucial events of my past.

In the basement, dark and light seem to swirl together, the light filtering in through two narrow windows, the dark unwilling to give up its hold over the corners, or the boxes it creeps along. Our teenaged uncle, Peter, pushes my little brothers around. Their arms and legs look like a tangle of branches, a net I don't want to get caught inside. I back into one of the dark corners, hoping to disappear. Peter grabs Mark's three-year-old hand and places it on his bare penis, holding it there. The air seems thick with the smell of burnt rubber and the speckled patterns of light and dark. I want to make my brothers disappear too, the three of us gone from here in a flash that will erase the dark and light patterns, the smell of mould and rubber. But Peter finds me in the dark, pushes my face against his penis, forcing it into my mouth. I gag, falling back against the wall.

At the college clinic, I'd asked for a pregnancy test in the calm voice I'd rehearsed on my way over, in words determined not to frighten or upset me, in words that distanced me from the stereotypes and statistics of teenage pregnancy—those girls who didn't know about birth control, who were poor or ignorant, neglected or abused. I was holding tight to the myth of a normal, happy childhood, having forgotten the ways Peter had hurt my brothers and me when we were small.

Two days after the blood test, I sat across from the doctor who tapped her pen gently and repeatedly against her coffee mug and said, "You're pregnant."

As if those words by themselves meant nothing, I waited for her to continue.

Her grey eyes were soft and serious like those of a good teacher who wants to make sure you understand a difficult math problem. "Your last period was the end of June, which makes you eight weeks along. You have options," she said, her pen now poised in the air.

I nodded, holding her gaze. Under my stolid surface, I had a sense of inevitability, felt wooed by the idea of fate wielding a brush over my as yet empty canvas, outlining the future I'd been unable to conjure.

"You're sixteen so you can get an abortion in New York State without your parents' permission. It won't be difficult to arrange. You should probably have it done next week."

"I don't want an abortion," I said. Just thinking of it felt like a denial of the depth of my feelings for Joseph, and of the germ of adult identity I'd created for myself by falling in love.

"Give it some thought. If you're still sure you don't want an abortion, talk to your parents. Then come back and see me. If you decide to see the pregnancy to term, we happen to have a midwife on staff this year." The doctor set her pen down on the desk, her concerned expression relaxing into a smile at the serendipity of the midwife's presence, a reminder that things could sometimes turn out for the best.

That evening, I sat on the dark, well-worn bench in the dormitory's only telephone booth. I'd told Joseph I'd call as soon as I knew. He was studying chemical engineering at the University of Toronto. For days he'd been waiting to hear about the test, to discover how my body might affect his well-planned, clearly visible future.

The news seemed to surprise him, but I'd known we wouldn't get away with our careless nights. My body had been warning me for months. That winter and spring, I'd had stomach flu three times, reacting to the stresses of being in love and sexually active, but unable to understand why love was making me feel sick.

"Are you sure?" Joseph asked for a second time.

"I had the test. The doctor was sure."

In the silence that followed I felt the muscles around my belly tighten.

"What are we going to do?"

He seemed to be asking himself, searching for the right answer to the problem, like he'd done when we sat next to each other in calculus class. At first I'd been able to solve the differential equations as well as he could, but once Joseph and I started having sex, I lost my ability to understand the problems. I thought I was bad at calculus, but now I can see that I was uncomfortable competing with my boyfriend, and that being sexually active made me feel smaller and less capable, like the little girl in the basement.

"The doctor said I can get an abortion, but I don't want that," I said.

"Have you told your parents?"

"No. I'm scared." What I felt was, if I tell them, it will be real. It will move outside the secret world he and I have defined with our two joined bodies.

"We both need to talk to our parents," said Joseph. "You'll feel better once you've told them."

I dialled my parents' number, the warm black receiver tucked under my chin. My heart pounded. I had seldom disappointed my mother and father, had been a careful daughter, obeying the rules despite my mishaps and miscalculations. This had been my year of rebellion, not against my parents, who pretty much let me come and go as I wished, but against myself, the persona I'd developed of a quiet, studious girl ever anxious to please.

Now that I should be most adult, waiting for my parents to answer the phone, the hopeful, independent Kim seemed to have disappeared. I felt punished, subdued, quaking at the sound of my mother's "hello."

"I'm pregnant."

The words crackled through the phone lines to meet silence. After a moment my mother said something about an abortion. She sounded distant, lost. I hadn't expected to wound her, hadn't thought how my actions might affect others.

"I don't think so," I said, impatient because I'd made my decision.

Twisting the long black cord around my hand, I could feel my mother's concern wrap around me. She was afraid that I wouldn't be able to handle being a mother when I was still so much a daughter, that life was more difficult than I had so far imagined.

"Have you told Joe?" she asked. My mother liked Joseph's friend-liness, humour, and pragmatism. When he broke his wrist sailing, he came to our house first, for comfort, and my mother drove him to the hospital even though it was just a short walk down the road.

"He knows," I said, not wanting to discuss Joseph with her.

My father's liking for Joseph had been tempered with resentment and competition; he hadn't been ready for his only daughter to love another man. A few years later when my parents separated, my father blamed Joseph for the distance that grew between him and me. But Joseph had nothing to do with the distance, which had sprouted from my own anger and feelings of rejection, and from the guilt my father had been unable to shrug off.

That night when my father came on the line, his warm voice brought out the tears I'd been holding back. I relaxed into the wooden bench as if he were telling me a bedtime story. He didn't approve of abortion. I was doing the right thing—keeping the baby. Everything would be okay. I nodded noiselessly into the phone, blew my nose and murmured that I was fine.

"I guess these things don't always happen to other people," he said.

My parents didn't know that my brothers and I had been molested by our uncle. Peter was my father's youngest brother, and only eight years older than I was. When we visited our grandparents on Sunday afternoons, my parents told us to go play with Peter, never guessing what he did to us in the basement, how he made us feel trapped, helpless, and guilty. We never told because we were afraid that Peter might find more ways to hurt us. We never told because we were afraid our parents would be angry with us, because as much as we were afraid of Peter, we were also fascinated by his urgent commands, the things he made us do, the awe and contempt we felt for him, and for our own small bodies. We never told because the darkness in that basement seemed unconnected with our daylight lives, and as long as we kept it a secret, we could pretend that it wasn't real, could forget that it had ever happened.

The next weekend, Joseph came to visit me to discuss our future. We ate dinner in the Alumnae House, where he'd taken a room and where we slept the night together for the first time, and bathed together in the big claw-footed bathtub. The food tasted fresh and satisfying after the chemical smells of the cafeteria. Sitting there across from Joseph I remembered the restaurant where he'd taken me one Saturday night in Bermuda. He'd looked handsome in a suit jacket and turtleneck. I'd worn a dress and angora sweater. We'd ordered wine like adults.

Joseph didn't try to dissuade me from keeping the baby but warned that his mother, Maria, was planning a visit to talk me into having an abortion. For weeks, I anxiously awaited news of her arrival, imagining her tall, elegantly suited figure bustling up the stairs and through my door.

"She's coming this weekend," Joseph said one day on the phone. "She'll be in New York."

"What day will she be here?"

"I don't know. Whenever she gets a chance."

"I may be out all weekend," I decided then and there.

"Don't be. She won't bite."

"Oh yeah? She hates me."

"No, she doesn't. She's concerned."

"About *you*," I retorted.

His mother scared me. I'd felt her disapproval the first time I met her at their house on the harbour. She was wearing a long wraparound skirt, green and blue, her pale hair pinned back, a cocktail tinkling in her hand. They were expecting company and I wasn't it.

"So this is your little friend," she said to Joseph.

Maria never showed up at my dorm that weekend. Maybe she realized the futility of her errand. Maybe she was too distraught to trust herself with me. Never once have I imagined she thought better of it, accepting what Joseph and I were sure to do. I was ruining her son's life. That's how she would have seen it. She was a passionate woman. I can still envision her red face, her clenched fists, her voice saying, "I'd like to throttle her!" I never got over my shyness with her, but when she died of a stroke just seven years later, her partner assured me that she'd been proud of me—how I'd persisted in my studies and taken good care of Kristine. Maybe she never visited that long ago fall because she'd been busy with her own distractions—a deteriorating marriage, a new love affair.

She did come to Joseph's father's house in Toronto the first weekend in October for a meeting between our two families—Joseph, me, my parents, his father and stepmother, his mother. I don't remember if anyone else was there. I'd forgotten about that meeting until rereading the old letters and cards my mother gave me a couple of years ago. When I slid a Christmas card from its yellowed envelope, I was surprised to see that it was from Maria, apologizing for being hard on me in Toronto, saying, "But I was full of fear for the future for both of you," signing it, "All my love: Joseph's mother." I smiled at her signature. Had "Maria" seemed too friendly and "Mrs. Wilkinson" too stiff? Or had she wanted to remind me that she was still, and always would be, Joseph's mother?

Once I'd begun to remember the meeting, I could recall her storming out, but not what was said. It no longer seems to matter now that I'm older than Maria was back then, now that I realize just how young and naive Joseph and I had been, now that I recognize what we were giving up by taking on such adult responsibilities, now that I know how it feels to worry about grown children, to want their lives to be easier, lighter.

When my college roommate developed a sudden friendship with a girl from New Jersey and asked if I'd mind trading rooms with her, I agreed, thinking my surroundings made little difference to me. But when I moved down the hall to the smaller, darker room, farther from the convenience of phone and washroom, I felt duped. I didn't feel that way for long. My new roommate, Darla, welcomed me with a bubbly enthusiasm that made the room homey and comforting. I hung my creeping charlie in the smaller, north-facing window, tacked photos to the corkboard over my bed, yet still sat on my secret, keeping a big part of me hidden, even from my new friend.

Darla dragged me to parties, found a small refrigerator for our room, took me grocery shopping. Her boyfriend, Daniel, who played guitar and dreamed of a career in music, seemed happy to include me in their dinners and conversations. Sometimes, at night, I fell asleep to the discreet sounds of their lovemaking.

In the mornings, I picked up my mail on my way to the coffee shop for breakfast, avoiding the busy cafeteria whenever I could. My mother used to send me long letters full of family news and concern, urging me to "write or tell us your feelings about things. Write and tell us your plans and what you want. Keep cheerful, be happy. We love you." One day, I'd sat down to my eggs and bagel with a letter from my grandmother. The thin airmail paper rustling in my hands, I'd read, "If you were my sixteen-year-old daughter I'd have taken you to a hospital and got you a D&C—and let you get on with your education. I've lived long enough to know you have to be practical in things like this. Hope things turn out for the best—never can tell."

I've always remembered my grandmother's pragmatic outburst, but when I discovered her letter again a couple of years ago, I was surprised that she hadn't mentioned my predicament until the fourth page, after an account of visiting a bargain outlet called the Crazy Teepee and before her plans to look for partridge berries. I was also touched by how supportive her letter was. Like my mother's, it was full of a kindness my adolescent self either took for granted or was unable to acknowledge. Back then, I noticed only that all the women seemed to be saying I'd made the wrong choice, but what other examples had they set? My mother and her mother married at nineteen, my father's mother at sixteen like me.

When I went back to school at forty for an MFA in writing, I asked my mother, who'd never gone to college, if she'd ever thought of taking university courses.

"What for?" she said, her voice rising in astonishment and scorn at the idea of herself as a mature student writing tests and papers. "I never liked that part of school."

But lately, she's been going to art classes. With a mixture of pride and self-deprecation, she tells me what her art teacher says about her paintings. My mother has always been a passionate phone doodler but she never knew she could paint. That leads me to wonder if there are other things she'd enjoy, other things she never knew she could do.

By mid-October, the campus maples had turned yellow, red, and orange. Growing up in Bermuda, I'd never experienced a real autumn.

Part of me delighted in the dramatic change, the brilliant and varied fall colours, but the other part, lonely for Joseph and my family, saw only that the leaves were dying and the days slowly darkening. As I soaped my thickening belly in the mouldy shower stall, queasily chewed a tuna sandwich in the cafeteria, or ducked through the rain between classes, I felt I was paying for the fun I'd had during my senior year of high school—the new friends, the parties, the giddy freedom of driving a moped, the heady new drugs of love and sex. In the space of a summer, I seemed to have plunged from light to dark, from warmth to cold, from love to loneliness.

Afternoons, on my way to Spanish class, I kicked through leaves that lay bright and deep across campus, feeling them drag against my ankles like a dry surf as I silently recited the lines of Hopkins's "Spring and Fall," a poem I'd read a year before in English class but was only now beginning to understand.

> Margaret, are you grieving
> Over Goldengrove unleaving?
> . . . as the heart grows older
> It will come to such sights colder
> By and by, nor spare a sigh
> Though worlds of wanwood leafmeal lie . . .†

If Hopkins's poem provided a rhythm for my grief, the earthy rot of fallen leaves gave it a fragrance. Even though I had a boyfriend who told me I was beautiful, I didn't believe it. I compared myself to other girls who seemed prettier, more popular, who knew how to dress and what to say. I wanted to memorize the leaves' shapes and colours, to incorporate them within myself just as I'd absorbed the words of the poem, as if its beauty could make me beautiful, as if its design could give my awkward, unworthy life shape.

꙾ Kicking through the fallen leaves, I found myself counting over the happier days of childhood like the red beads on the abacus we once used in math class, unaware that my grief echoed an earlier grief over a loss I'd forgotten—the loss of my virginity when I was seven and my uncle Peter plunged a finger through my hymen. He'd been babysitting me and my brothers while our parents went out to dinner. The next day, my brothers told my mother that Peter had shown us his penis. I told her I never wanted him to babysit again. After that, we stayed away from our grandparents' basement, and soon forgot the things that had happened there, our daylight lives reasserting themselves, our memories seeping underground like rainwater collecting in a cave.

My happy childhood was a pretty story I told myself, a dream I didn't want to wake from because my dreaminess protected me from the past, but it also made me short-sighted about the future, left me tripping over my own feet.

Now I think that I recoiled from the idea of having an abortion partly because it seemed like another invasion that would leave me feeling bruised and battered like the one nine years earlier I was trying hard not to remember. Whatever instinct I was following, whether of the body or the emotions, I chose to keep the baby, dreamy with fantasies of single-motherhood in the apartments just outside campus. But one evening Joseph phoned to ask me to marry him, and I said yes.

꙾ When I returned to the dorm after my wedding in Toronto, hauling my suitcase up the three flights of stairs to my room to avoid the lurch of the service elevator, one look at Darla's friendly face made me feel the press of tears I'd been holding back all day.

I stared at the limp freesias lying on the corn-coloured Amelia Earhart suitcase bought to celebrate my departure for college. Yesterday, the freesias had been part of my bridal bouquet, along with white rosebuds, just beginning to open. The bouquet had arrived in a big white box with corsages for the women in the wedding party, and flowers for the luncheon afterwards. Joseph's mother had decided not to attend. His father and stepmother had arranged everything, including a buffet at their house and a big cake with KIM & JOSEPH declared in dark chocolate on a slab of wavy white marzipan.

I told Darla that I was pregnant and had just married Joseph. I told her how morning sickness had made me vomit in his father's Cadillac on my way to city hall, how Joseph's aunt had draped her fur coat over my shoulders as I climbed out of the car, and how seeing my thirteen-year-old brother Mark wearing a yellow Tarzan tie for my wedding had made me wish we were little kids again.

Darla hugged me, and later returned from a weekend visit home with a kosher chicken her mother had sent for me. She cooked it in the communal kitchen downstairs, where it smelled like pure essence of chicken. As my piece of bread sopped up the gravy, I felt steeped in affection.

One night, when Darla and Daniel were out at a college dance, the dorm felt hushed and empty. I opened the window, inhaling the fresh mild scent of the November evening, and searching for signs of life on campus. But I couldn't see or hear a soul. I rummaged in my desk for a big brown envelope, pulling out the poems and scraps of stories I'd been writing since I was fourteen. I read through them, carefully laying each sheet of paper onto the last, as if hoping that together they might add up to something. Then I stuffed the papers back into their envelope, and dropped them into the garbage bin that sat outside our room.

A few minutes later, stretched out on my bed, one hand resting on my hardening belly, the other pressed to the wall that separated me from the hallway where my poems lay amid empty beer bottles and the crumpled false starts of essays, I was surprised by a knock on the door. For one crazy moment, I thought someone had found my writings, recognized their worth, and was restoring them to me. But it was the girl from a few doors down, who liked Sinatra and whose room was always filled with candles.

"Lena caught a burglar rummaging through her drawers," she said. "He must have thought everyone would be at the dance. You'd better lock your door."

But I wasn't worried about the burglar. How could I be when I was trying hard not to think of what Peter had stolen from me, or what the baby inside was taking every day, siphoning off from my bloodstream, or what I'd given to Joseph along with my love, or what I'd thrown out with the garbage? What dreams and musings, which particles of myself would I never see again?

As I locked the door behind the girl with the candles, I felt safe with her roaming the hallways looking out for us date-less, dance-less girls. I held onto the plain gold wedding band that encircled my ring finger, but that I mostly kept in the drawer beside my bed. It made me feel safe too, as did knowing that my poems were stashed where no one would ever read them and discover how hopeful I'd been.

I thought then that becoming a mother meant I had to deny other aspects of myself, like the ambitious girl who dreamed of being a writer, and the party girl who craved fun and attention. The party girl would have chosen to have an abortion, then dulled her pain by smoking weed, drinking beer, and stumbling into the beds of random men.

A few years later, when I started to write again, this phantom self showed up in my first complete short story. She rises from a rain puddle, seeping into the protagonist's ordered but unhappy domestic life, displacing her. Oddly, the party girl with her brash belief in fun is better able to handle married life and motherhood than the weary protagonist, who wishes herself away from husband and kids but has no clear sense of who she might be without them.

Early December, five months pregnant and starting to show, I visited my friend, Heather, at her college in Rhode Island. From the plane, the bare trees looked like pale silver grasses against a dark ground. Having flown into Boston, I caught the bus to Providence, arriving sleepy and nauseous from the bus's bump and sway. Over the past couple of years, Heather had spent many weeks living with my family while her parents went to England to consult specialists about her father's heart condition, and while he had surgery there. We had grown used to sharing not only a room, but also our dreams and fears.

Heather picked me up in someone's car. After we ate dinner and met her friends, I slept on a borrowed mattress on the floor of her small dorm room. The voices of Billy Joel and Paul Anka crooned from next door.

In the morning, we drove to the mall with two other girls. The conversation about cute guys and clothes made me feel strange, light-headed, or maybe it was the stuffy mall air, the fluorescent lights. That night we sat in the common room, watching *Holiday Inn*, mesmerized by the prettiness of the New England inn, the energy of the dance numbers, the corny inevitability of the love story, how love promised to cure Bing's slick, urban soul.

Saturday morning, Paul Anka sang again from next door—"You're having my baby." I cringed at the words, at the idea that Heather might think I was identifying with them. I wished they had never been written, that I could forget for one minute that my body and my life were altered forever. As I sat on the mattress, fastening a bra over my newly large and blue-veined breasts, Heather said, "Just because you're pregnant, doesn't mean you're a woman yet."

I knew she was driven to this outburst by the fear of change, the fear that we were moving away from each other. I also knew that she was right. But I'd spent the better part of the fall counting over my childhood memories, saying goodbye, because I *was* a woman, even though a big part of me was still afraid of what womanhood would bring.

I longed for and dreaded the end of the fall term at college. My pregnant belly was expanding with each passing week, pushing me further from the other students. I saw myself trapped inside a big bubble that was carrying me away from our breathless discussions about Paul Simon's guitar playing and the existence of God, carrying me away from the parties, classes, and love affairs that lay ahead for them, knowing that, even though I was the one who wouldn't be here next term, they were the ones who were leaving me behind.

Later that night, I woke to the sound of Darla giggling. A cool breeze from the open window teased my nose with the earthy aroma of weed, but I drifted back to sleep. In the morning, the room felt cold. Pulling on beige corduroys and a brown sweater, I noticed my creeping charlie—a dark, soggy mess on the windowsill. Darla apologized—she'd thought it needed fresh air. On my way to class, I dropped it into the big black garbage pail. I would be leaving in a couple of weeks and wouldn't have been able to take it with me on the plane. Still, I felt negligent. I'd bought the plant for the bright morning sun of my first room, where its leaves had sparkled as if making up for the lack of conversation. In Darla's room, I'd only noticed it when it was already thirsting for water. What kind of mother did that make me? Would I pay attention to my baby only when she cried?

When my father arrived to pick me up from college, Darla had already gone home for the holidays, but her boyfriend Daniel was waiting in my dorm room with me, sitting on the desk chair while I sat on the bare bed holding the card he'd just given me. In his spidery handwriting, he'd quoted Simon and Garfunkel: "Sail on Silver Girl. Sail on by. Your time has come to shine. All your dreams are on their way." I wonder now if Daniel knew that I was pregnant. I'd told Darla not to tell anyone, but it must have become obvious by then, although judging from Daniel's card, he didn't seem to realize how far away my dreams had felt. I could see them sailing off without me, just as he and Darla would soon be heading back to school without me in January, and then on with their separately unfolding lives.

Darla had already moved her stuff to the room she'd be sharing with another friend next term. The shelf where she'd kept her tape player and the cassettes I used to listen to while doing my Spanish homework was empty, the corner where our small refrigerator once sat humming was wispy with spiderwebs, and the desks, once piled with books, were bare.

My father shook Daniel's offered hand, leaning over him a little to assert his greater height.

"Good to meet you, Mr. Aubrey," Daniel said.

"Are you ready, Kim?" my father asked.

"Can I help with your suitcase?" asked Daniel.

"I've got it," said my father, gripping the handle.

I wanted to stay chatting with Daniel, warding off my future, but I pulled on my suede coat, grabbed my backpack, and glanced once more around the empty room, which no longer smelled of shampoo and apples, but of dry wood and dust.

"I wonder if anyone will be living here next term," I said.

"Write to me," Daniel said, hugging me goodbye.

We did write to each other once or twice. He sent me a glossy photo he took of Rio de Janeiro at sunset. I sent him a thank-you card. By January, everyone knew that I'd dropped out because I was pregnant. A rumour spread that Daniel was the father. Darla wrote to tell me that he was having a bad winter, upset by the rumours and in pain from a broken leg. I let his friendship, something I could have used more of back then, slip away.

Safely out of my life, Daniel became my "what if" guy, the musician who read books and appreciated art, while Joseph was the engineering student who made fun of "artsies." I used to fantasize conversations with Daniel about a book I was reading, or an idea that had come to me in the night. Imagining what it would have been like to live with someone different was easier than asking, What if I'd never gotten pregnant? What if I hadn't married? What if I hadn't kept the baby?

꧁ The summer after Kristine was born, Darla visited us at my parents' New Hampshire cottage. Her new boyfriend was at a friend's house in the nearby city. I was staying with my parents for a month while Joseph spent time with his mother in Bermuda, but mostly went boating and partied with our old friends. I felt left out, left behind. Seeing Darla didn't help. She'd met new people, was working in Boston. We didn't have much to talk about. She seemed surprised whenever I went to my room to nurse the baby. I worried that she must think my family old-fashioned and repressed. When we drove her to meet her boyfriend, he stared at us in our rented station wagon as if we were aliens landing our silver craft on the hot city street. Darla and I hugged goodbye. From the back seat of the car, I watched her join her friends. She looked glamorous and exotic in faded jeans, Indian blouse, and sandals. I sat next to Kristine, who was buckled into her baby seat. My right breast leaked through the nursing bra, darkening the red of my T-shirt.

꧁ When Kristine was six months old, I went back to school, taking a linguistics class at the University of Toronto. I'd make dinner Monday evenings, feed the baby, and eat with Joseph before grabbing my books and walking across campus to the busy social sciences building where I'd sit taking notes, blending in with the other first-year students. No one there, not even the professor, knew that I was a mother. Just as none of the mothers in our apartment building knew that I was not yet eighteen. I wanted to keep my life as student and my life as mother and wife separate because they didn't seem to make sense together. In linguistics, I learned to label each syllable with its phonetic symbol, each word with its syntactical function. My own roles weren't as easy to classify or understand.

꧁ Even though I spent many years of my life attending university part-time while raising my daughters, earning a bachelor's degree and then a master's in English literature, I always felt separate from the other students, always missed the college life I'd left behind when I was seventeen. Then two years ago, after finally allowing myself to face how childhood trauma had affected my life, after talk therapy and other modes of healing, I enrolled in a low-residency MFA program in Vermont.

Settling into a dorm twenty-four years after my first aborted college experience, I made my single bed with the college-issued white sheets, hung my summer skirts and pants in the closet, stacked a few novels on the shelf along with my vitamins and face creams, and went to dinner in the cafeteria with a young woman whose room was across the hall from mine.

I felt strange away from Joseph and my daughters, but also triumphant, as I stood in line in the bustling cafeteria, which smelled so much better than the one I'd eaten in as a teenager, selecting the savoury tempeh steaks I'd never cook at home because Joseph wouldn't touch them, or ate breakfast with people I'd just met, exchanging thoughts about last night's poetry reading, or braved the basement laundry room to wash clothes for myself alone, no longer hiding in my room as I'd done my first time in college, but joining the other writing students in the dorm lounge or on the grassy quad, where we shared our hopes and fears, prepared for another day of lectures and workshops, and developed sudden, lasting friendships.

What I'd lost getting pregnant, marrying, and having a baby at such a young age couldn't be recaptured, but the MFA residencies did restore some of that youthful buoyancy, that feeling that my life as an adult was just beginning, and that I could shape it in some ways. It helped me to regain the sense of agency I'd lost when my uncle molested me, and to counter my old belief that I had no choice but to sit back and let life happen.

Of course, in becoming a mother, I'd gained a lot too—my kids had helped me to feel safe, had given me a sense of purpose and meaning, had grounded me when I needed to be grounded, when as much as I'd longed to let loose and fly off on my own, I hadn't possessed the ballast for it, would have floated away like a sheaf of papers on the wind, like the protagonist in my short story, "The Puddlewoman," who not only loses her family to the party girl, but finds herself diminished without them.

🪶 Now, saying goodbye to Kathryn at her dorm and driving with Joseph back to our empty house, I feel grief-stricken and lost; a big part of my life, that part that began when I found myself pregnant with Kristine all those years ago, is ending and, once again, I feel left behind. But the next day, I sit at my desk revising one of the stories I wrote for my MFA thesis, and thinking about my last college residency, just two months ago—how my friends and I attended each other's lectures and readings, how we picked up dinner from the bustling cafeteria and ate it outside, resuming conversations we'd begun at breakfast or in workshop. How we sat together on the grassy quad, the night before Independence Day, reminiscing about the week's adventures, which had already become part of our shared language. Watching fireworks splash up into the sky, then fall back like drops of coloured water, brightening the dark rim of trees.

KIM AUBREY is a Saskatoon writer who has an MFA in writing from Vermont College. Her stories, essays, and poems have appeared in journals and anthologies, including *Event*, *Room*, *upstreet*, *Numero Cinq*, and *Best Canadian Stories*. Kim is associate fiction and non-fiction editor for *Grain* magazine and a founding member and editor of Red Claw Press. Kim grew up in Bermuda, where she leads an annual writers' retreat. She is currently working on a graphic memoir.

†Gerard Manley Hopkins, "Spring and Fall," *Poems of Gerard Manley Hopkins Now First Published*, ed. Robert Bridges (London: Humphrey Milford, 1918).

Dead Baby, Imperfect Baby
A MEDITATION WITH DOLLS

CATHY STONEHOUSE

I

In the FAO Schwarz newborn nursery, smiling, silent babies are lined up in rows. Nurses in crisp white uniforms hover in attendance, ready to offer advice to aspiring parents. Most of the babies are white, but a few are "ethnic," brown-skinned or with Asian features. The babies are all perfect, and all plastic. According to the FAO Schwarz website, the nursery offers "beautiful and realistic babies that girls treasure . . . babies that look and FEEL like real infants." The infants all come with names and birth certificates and can be kitted out with cribs, bedding, clothing, diapers, and feeding supplies before their eager mothers leave the store.

II

When I was about five, my father came home with a present for me. It was a Tiny Tears doll, dressed in a pink dress, pink corduroy jacket and bonnet, and pink shoes. I called her Tina. I fed her white liquid from a pretend baby bottle, as well as water, which would immediately come out of her eyes as tears, and a few seconds later out of a hole approximately where her vagina should have been. At some point I stuffed something up her vagina so the hole was blocked but she still cried.

III

Female mannequins were originally religious in purpose, but at some point began being made for children. Dolls for play are now part of most of the world's cultures. The baby doll was first introduced in 1851 in England, as part of Queen Victoria's Great Exhibition. Baby dolls were most popular between the early 1900s and the 1950s, at which point the fashion doll took the upper hand. Today, baby dolls are marketed mostly at younger children, in particular the under sevens. Baby dolls do not come in for as much cultural criticism as fashion dolls such as Bratz or Monster High mannequins, which are often blamed for promoting the sexualization of young girls. Nevertheless they bring with them their own implicit moral complexity.

IV

When my sister-in-law gave me a baby doll and doll stroller for my daughter F's second birthday, I was torn. Was giving her dolls a form of gender conditioning? I hid them away and put off giving them to her for as long as I could. Eventually I broke down and rapidly the first baby doll was joined by a second and the two were christened Bowie and Cheetah. Much better names than I ever came up with, although no one, not even F, could ever quite figure out which was which. Luckily it didn't matter. One was slightly larger, the other newer. Both had eyes that opened and closed, and soft bodies. They answered happily to either name.

Then, around about F's fourth birthday, the Barbie question came up. I said no, but caved less than a week later, purchasing the most innocuous set I could find — one that came with a horse, "farmer Barbie," as F christened her, although the horse quickly disappeared. In short order, four or five others appeared, along with those familiar little high-heeled plastic shoes. My sister-in-law also soon obliged by dispatching an assemblage of Barbie clothing collected up from the females of the family, none of whom were any longer of Barbie doll age, and soon our living room was littered with minuscule neon pink miniskirts and lime green fun-fur legwarmers.

V

As a child I was most fond of Tina and her "big sister," Karen, a doll whose arms and legs could be made to walk. Karen had satiny blond ringlets. She and Tina went to my grandmother's once for a short holiday and came home with perfect new, pink dresses, knitted coats and hats. I also had a larger doll who "talked," if you pulled a cord in her back. She wore a green dress and was called Linda. I never really warmed to her, to tell the truth. I also had a scruffy girl doll named Biddy, whose greenish-brown hair was matted. I scribbled on her body in felt pen and would occasionally punish her by stripping her and "locking" her in a dark cupboard by herself.

VI

I "lost" (weird word) my first child, a daughter, after five months in utero. Too far along to be considered a miscarriage, yet not far along enough to be stillborn. She didn't just die. We killed her—well, sort of. My partner and I agreed that I should undergo a late term abortion because our daughter had a particular genetic abnormality that meant her chances of survival, to birth or beyond it, were extremely low. The list of her possible afflictions was lengthy and sobering, every system in her body potentially affected. Nevertheless she did not die from her condition. We induced her death by inducing her birth.

Her birth/death was gentle and dignified. I opted to stay awake and birth her vaginally rather than being drugged and having her taken out. The whole process took just a few hours and ended with her sliding out into the toilet, or rather a bowl the nurse had placed there to catch her. There was pain, but not much; blood, but not much. My breasts produced milk, but not a lot, and it was barely a week before my belly shrank back. After she was born the nurses took her away, washed her and dressed her in a diminutive onesie, together with a hat, the kind real babies wear.

VII

The Christmas before Gracie died, the same sister-in-law who, five years later collected up the Barbie clothes, presented us with several garbage bags full of infant and baby gear collected from secondhand stores and church basement sales. By then, we did not know for certain Gracie had trisomy-18 but were pretty sure. Nevertheless, for some reason I can't quite remember, my husband and I sat through the presentation of the clothes and went through them dutifully, mouthing our thanks as we held each little sleeper up to the light.

One of my aunts lost a baby shortly after birth, the other experienced multiple miscarriages. The sister-in-law offering the baby clothes was once a twin but her sister died at birth. Yet my parents-in-law never talked about this, even to her. Such stories surface only when strictly necessary, after the fact, and never before.

The baby Jesus: a being who holds our terror of death and eats it. A doll wrapped in fabric; vinegar on a sponge. *And they wrapped him up in swaddling cloths and laid him in a manger, because there was no room for them, in the inn.*

VIII

After she was born, we sat and held Gracie for quite a few hours for she was real, all right, our flesh and blood offspring, although her body was dark, thin-skinned, and her eyes were closed. She was tiny, just about the length of my hand. Yet in every other way she was quite perfect: narrow fingers, whorled ears, the shape of her legs exactly that of my husband's. Okay, she was dead, but there was no sign of struggle. The doctor couldn't specify the moment she passed on. Her body cooled; she did not breathe. Eventually we had to give her up. But for those few hours she seemed complete. We snapped several photographs. The nurse took footprints. Look at this, I wanted to shout. Isn't she amazing?

IX

"I hope you understand," said my friend, turning her face away. "I just don't want to see. It's not personal." But it was personal. This was my child we were talking about.

"I hope you don't mind, but we decided not to tell X. We think she's too young," whispered my father-in-law. X being our niece who knew I was pregnant and was also old enough to become pregnant herself.

"Sorry for your loss," said the people, the cards.

No words or images existed for what we had been through. A perversion, a twist, a monstrosity; the silent, hushed-up world of death crashing helter-skelter into the nursery, as if someone had driven a hearse right into a daycare. Oops, sorry. There was a sense of embarrassment, of having inadvertently caused offence. A need to apologize: sorry. I just don't know what to say.

X

I can't remember what we dressed Gracie in, but I do remember we buried a teddy bear with her. Quite possibly a waste of a stuffie but it felt necessary, as did the casket and cremation of what was left of her (she decomposed quickly, as you might expect). The funeral director was from Britain, and chatty. En route to the crematorium he gave us the highlights of his many years in the profession, including the time he buried one of Jack the Ripper's victims (not the original killer, the 1970s one). It was January, cold and bleak. The lugubrious young man at the crematorium wore a white shirt and black pants, as if for a high school band performance. Afterwards I put away all the pregnancy books, stuffed the baby gear into a suitcase and shoved it under the bed. "You can always try again." There it all stayed for over a year.

XI

The babydoll is a mini negligee popularized by the 1956 movie *Baby Doll* starring Carroll Baker, who played the role of a teenage sex nymph. Babydolls are similar in style to the little dresses still manufactured for female babies, which come with matching knickers, otherwise known as rompers. I have never worn an adult babydoll, but I have dressed my daughter in rompers. One set came from Japan, where my husband and I lived for a year. It consisted of a white long-sleeved snap-up onesie with red polka dots, and a little red jumper to wear over the top.

In Japan there are shrines dedicated to Jizo, a Buddhist god, one of whose jobs is to take care of "water babies," those who die before they reach this world. He carries a stick, which the babies hold on to as he guides them over the river. All over Japan there are little Jizo shrines filled with stone statues that grieving parents dress in little red dresses and bibs.

In Japan, abortion is not controversial. "Water babies" are honoured whatever their circumstances. Japan also has a long history of doll-making. When we were there I visited a toy museum and purchased a book about Japanese dolls, which included the wooden *kokeshi* as well as more contemporary fashion and baby dolls. What wasn't included, of course, was the Japanese Love Doll, a sophisticated, life-size sex toy that can be rented by the hour or day by lonely gentlemen, provided they supply their own detachable "hole." This may seem repulsive to some, but what is the difference between such a fetish object and, for example, certain adult-oriented collector dolls, such as the more-real-than-real silicone infants that "actually breathe" when placed in your arms? When and how does a transitional object become a fetish, as opposed to a deity, and at what point does verisimilitude become down-right creepy? Is it easier to love the unborn, the undead?

XII

After losing Gracie, our lives continued, even though, at the time, it seemed they never would. Her official due date came and went and eventually we got her ashes (such as they were) back from the crematorium and planned to scatter them but kept putting it off. We weren't ready. We treated each other kindly but there was a hole. I heard about a woman who had other babies yet continued to talk about her first as if he were still living, setting a place for him at the dinner table and signing Christmas cards on his behalf. I did not do either, but neither did I let go entirely. What if we had waited, seen what would happen instead of taking her fate into our own hands? Would she have somehow, miraculously, proved us all wrong? Was she, in fact, healthy? I knew this was not true, but I could not stop wondering. Yet nor did I wish to wax saccharine, sentimental. Dead babies are not angels; nor are they fairies. They are just what they are: ex-beings, short-lived. I particularly recoiled at the words "it must have happened for a reason."

What reason would that be?

XIII

We did, in the end, *try again*. I conceived almost instantaneously and had a healthy pregnancy, which culminated in a drug-free home birth. The same doctor and midwives who had seen me through Gracie's coming and going also saw me through F's arrival.

The first year of her life was wonderful and yet exhausting. I had a terrible time breastfeeding at first, and just as that got sorted out she developed asthma, which meant none of us slept more than fifteen minutes at a time. By the time she was two, we were finally recovering, glad to enjoy what we had and not think too far ahead at least for a little while. Slowly most of the families we knew began to grow, yet somehow we couldn't quite muster the courage to *try again* again.

There were various reasons. Part of it was age. After having the risk statistics shoved in our faces, it was hard to forget that my and my husband's combined years put us in the spike zone, where the chance of genetic abnormalities begins to skyrocket. Part of it was fear. Faced with the same situation, how would we handle it, especially with F in the house?

Time passed, and soon third siblings began to appear. One day I went to the park with my six-year-old and met two moms from my old baby group who each suddenly had four apiece. The sight was a physical shock. I had to leave, quickly. Grief was catching up to me, heading straight for my jugular.

Where are my others? I asked. Where are my children? Gracie would have been almost eight, and if I'd been busy I could have had two others. I pictured them and gave them names. One girl, one boy. Zoe and Rowan.

But they weren't there.

My daughter was there. And yet this greed kept rising up. Slowly at first, then gaining strength as the years passed by, to the point that when the Sudanese child we had sponsored after Gracie died wrote us year after year about each of her brand new siblings, I felt jealous. How could that be? Here I was, my one child consuming my every moment and there they were, living twelve to a room, and I still felt hard done by. Then I got back in touch with an old housemate to discover she had birthed seven. Seven: all of them gorgeous, healthy, and talented. How wonderful. I hated her. I wanted some of that.

"You could adopt." That was everyone else's solution. Except it wasn't a solution, it was avoidance, a way to circumvent embarrassing grief. We did look into it, but to adopt publically would entail years and years of waiting unless we wanted a teenager, or a seven-year-old with learning difficulties, or a group of siblings, which we didn't, because we knew we couldn't handle it. Meanwhile, to adopt an infant privately was impossibly expensive. We simply didn't have the thousands of dollars required. I also felt morally confused by international adoption. I did not want to do harm with my greed. So instead of pursuing this further, we gave up. After all, we were already getting on, and we had a family, one that had almost not happened, and we didn't want to wreck it.

XIV

Two years ago I finally retrieved the few, select pieces of dollhouse furniture I had kept from my own dollhouse and gave them to F, to combine with hers. It was strange, even disconcerting, to finger the tiny, crimson upholstered sofa and armchair my dimly remembered doll family had sat on, their legs held stiffly out, in the living room, not to mention see the plastic wedding cake and jelly, the tiny yellow plate of fish and chips placed on another kitchen table, thirty years later, each still as blurry and as fresh. There was a touch of Miss Havisham about it. Cobwebs should have surrounded us both.

"Tell me about your old dolls, Mama."

I do so with pleasure. I tell her about my dollhouse, about Tina and Karen, and how round about the age of nine I graduated on to Sindy, the cheaper, British version of Barbie whose blond hair turned up at the ends. Sindy was modelled after teenage girls and appears younger, more gauche than Barbie. For a while she was marketed in North America but her brand did not last. Her face was chubby, slightly wide-eyed, her body a touch less bizarrely proportioned than Barbie's.

My Sindy arrived in a green and yellow houndstooth miniskirt and knee-high yellow boots. I also at some point received a Sindy horse and riding outfit, and posed Sindy with both in our back lane. I still have the photograph. It smells slightly acidic, like an Instamatic. Yet ultimately, playing with Sindy was less compelling than playing with Tina. It mostly consisted of endlessly changing her clothes, clothes I can barely remember now, only their smallness. Tiny kitten heels, a snap-up miniskirt . . . there would be a moment of pleasure once the outfit was on at last, but then once again dissatisfaction set in.

That was the point. Sindy, Barbie, and collector toys in general are a consumerist rehearsal. Everything looks so gorgeous in the catalogue or packaging but somehow loses its lustre once merely owned. The clothes themselves, designed for "every occasion," are rehearsals also, selves to be mixed and matched, assembled and disassembled without risk. Luckily children do not always play with dolls the way they are "supposed to." Young girls manipulate the sexualized bodies of Barbies to enact familiar encounters at preschool, play dates, and bedtimes, without much regard for the dolls' proportions or clothes. And what teenage girl has never popped off a Barbie head and sent it flying?

XV

In Quesnel, there is a famous doll, a haunted doll. Her name is Mandy. Her face is cracked and bruised looking, yet she sits still in a corner of the city museum, looking out over its strange miscellany of objects: dentists' chairs; logging machinery, record players. They say her eyes follow you around the room. When we visited, I felt scared of her but also oddly empathetic. Whatever unresolved experiences she holds, they seem like a child's—and how easily we make children into ghosts, throwing our disowned feelings onto them, whether these are feelings of hope or terror. A child who commits a crime is too often regarded with hatred, no matter what the extenuating circumstances—witness the response of the British public to the two ten-year-old boys who were found guilty of murdering two-year-old James Bulger in 1993. Haunted dolls are also a staple of horror movies. They are lifelike yet not alive, and in this way they mediate between the living and the dead, haunt us with ambivalence, just as the "evil" child confuses innocence and experience. Robots, automata, dolls, and photographs all hold something of the living, and there are names for the fear of each one of them. The word for a fear of dolls is pediophobia. The word for a fear of children is pedophobia, a condition that can include specific fears of newborns, pregnancy, and fetuses.

XVI

My mother used to "dress" me for years. She was an absolute stickler for matching. Every item had to be colour coordinated, no matter how humble (we were not rich). Even today she waxes lyrical about my childhood clothing. "Do you remember that sundress, the one I made for you, with the ruched shoulder straps . . . ?" And the thing is, I do. Just as I remember the yellow cotton romper suit I put my daughter in the summer she was almost a year old. Just as I remember Sindy's yellow ribbed turtleneck, and the way it snapped together up the back.

I thought I would be such a non-consumerist parent, so very feminist and uncontaminated. Yet before I knew it I was buying up little baby clothes, toddler and preschooler outfits, "dressing" my daughter as if she were almost, well, a doll. I did my best to deny it. But somehow she learned when and how to look "pretty," and it certainly wasn't from her dad. These days her style involves wildly clashing patterns, styles, and colours, all worn with panache. Mostly I don't comment, but sometimes we get into tussles, usually over, of all things, jeans. I wear them almost every day ("Why don't you wear dresses, Mama?"), whereas my daughter hates them, would wear fleece leggings every day if she could.

As a child I dressed my dolls in items of clothing I myself had worn as an infant. Now my daughter does the same, and even dresses her dolls in my old hand-me-downs. There's something slightly sad about seeing Bowie or Cheetah wrapped up in the exquisite, hand-knitted matinee jackets and beribboned bonnets we got given for F by eager, elderly friends and relatives but that, for reasons of practicality (fleece really is better), she never wore. It's as if their good wishes for her are being binned. But they belong to another era, those bonnets and jackets, as do the little bootees and even the blankets. No one wraps their baby in a blanket these days, for fear of asphyxiation. Luckily, Bowie and Cheetah do not breathe.

Yet for those of us who go wibbly-wobbly at the sight of miniatures, there's nothing more *adorable* than attending a baby shower: mountains of crinkly pink, blue, or yellow tissue paper sticking out of soother-patterned bags that contain tiny outfits, little costumes for a person who has not yet been born: fake sneakers, fake jeans, unbelievably sweet little mini-dresses alongside the more sober, necessary items—diaper bags, breast pumps and bottle warmers, sleep sacks, waterproof pants, baby carriers—stocking up for a first child is a serious business. Most pregnancy books list thirty to fifty items as must-haves for the average expecting parent. And that's not including the inevitable *Aw* purchase, that cute-factor multiplier that incites oxytocin production in even the most unsentimental of observers—the panda bear costume, the diminutive tuxedo.

XVII

We scattered Gracie's ashes in Pacific Rim National Park, dropped them into a deep tidal pool to dissolve alongside sea stars and anemones and eventually be flung wide by the ocean. I keep a photo of the place near my desk. I also keep the drawing F made of me when she was four, a picture of a smiling woman seated before a computer screen with a steaming cup beside her, and the bright yellow flyer for Miniature World.

XVIII

Miniature World is located in the basement of the Empress Hotel in Victoria. I have visited numerous times. The last time was with F, on a mom and daughter visit to our provincial capital, when we bought tickets to the attraction and returned three times in one day. Miniature World features a series of dioramas, some very old and dusty, others more recent, in various scales and sizes, on historical, literary, and geographic themes. The dioramas are displayed in glass cases. There is also a large selection of dollhouses, some of which are modelled on real mansions at specific historical moments.

Viewing the dioramas is satisfying yet frustrating. It evokes a feeling of nostalgia as well as delight. The tiny worlds never quite let you in. They remain tantalizing, partial. Their smallness suggests distance, as if these are moments of experience seen in retrospect, or civilizations viewed from a great height. They are static, and therefore perfect, in that they will never dissolve or change. The wobbly, creaky nature of their machinery (Jack climbing up the beanstalk, a rotating carousel) serves only to underline this beauty, the slow, poignant winding down of life.

XIX

F is likely to outgrow her love of miniatures. She is likely to outgrow dolls. But for the meantime, I revel in it, this shared language of the magical, imaginary small. Together, we make paper dolls, collect stories about tiny people, and leave little openings for the possible to creep through. Yet I also know that dolls are totems, fetishes to cling to, to ward off grief. Not for children, perhaps, but certainly for adults, although childhood is full of loss and disappointment. Nevertheless, children's doll play is, most often, transforming. It moves experiences along and does not freeze them.

Some nights I wake, terrified at the thought of losing her, my live child, my beautiful, vulnerable heart, just the way I panic about my husband when he comes home late or forgets to call. If there is one aspect of mothering I never anticipated, it is this pain, this fear, and the constant loss, the tiny griefs as each stage of childhood finishes, even as what replaces them grows more profound. Perhaps that's why I take refuge in the miniature, hold onto it, even as I cringe.

"I think you like them more than I do, Mama," says F as I finger little pieces of furniture packaged up perfectly and hung in rows in the toy store.

"You're right," I agree. But I cannot quite tug myself away.

In my early twenties, I worked in London, England, for a pro-choice campaign, working to defend women's right to safe abortions. My boss (although we were, technically speaking, a collective), was a hard-bitten, lifetime campaigner, who often repeated how little regret she felt for her own abortions, insisting that there was nothing there yet to grieve.

These days I know that in her haste to assert women's rights she misrepresented the slippery nature of existence. Birth is as much a mystery as death is, and to me Gracie was *real*, a person, not just an idea. Yet she was also a placeholder, as expected children always are, an ideational pocket in which to stow hope. Perhaps this is why the anti-abortion movement flourishes, or at least one reason: the need to sanctify what is incipient and privilege it, to the point of absurdity, over what is. Once you are born you are mortal and specific, and grow more so with every passing year.

XX

"I wish I had a sister," says F, "but not brothers." One of her good friends has two older brothers, and she has seen how they don't get along.

"I know you do," I say, but I do not offer one.

The name on her bedroom door is hers, but recently she added her favourite doll's name: Taryn. This doll is a "girl" doll, not a baby doll, as close to a sister as she is going to get, at least at home. F gets Taryn up most days, and dresses her, spends hours talking to her, with the bedroom door closed. She has lots of friends, and these days sometimes they sleep over. But sometimes I still see ghosts around her, those of my imagined other children, Zoe and Rowan, as well as traces of all the children whose lives hang in the balance, both near and far.

Not all buds become flowers. Trees, flowers, field mice, dolphins, hyenas . . . all conceive, in their own way, offspring that perish. Some are merely unfertilized seeds. Others are runts eaten alive by their siblings, and even Jesus, presumably, was once a fetus. I wonder about the world F is growing up into, and how much of the "natural" there will be left. I try to teach her about justice and inequality, yet I know my own example leaves much to be desired. We are both works in progress. Meanwhile the doll babies keep watch, with their unseeing eyes, as night follows day in the FAO Schwarz nursery. In New York State, the child poverty rate is over twenty-six percent, the highest in the industrialized world.

CATHY STONEHOUSE is the author of a collection of short stories, *Something About the Animal* (Biblioasis, 2011), in addition to two collections of poetry, *The Words I Know* (Press Gang, 1994) and *Grace Shiver* (Inanna Publications, 2011). She also co-edited the Canadian creative nonfiction anthology *Double Lives: Writing and Motherhood* (McGill-Queen's University Press, 2008) along with Shannon Cowan and Fiona Tinwei Lam. She has one daughter.

THE POSSIBILITY
OF LOVE

Swan Song

CHRIS ARTHUR

I

I've often tried to write about Boll, but every time abandoned the attempt soon after starting, leaving a litter of scored-out sentences, pages quarter-filled, paper crumpled up and thrown away in frustration. Each time I come round to him I shy away at the last moment, like a nervous horse faced with the prospect of clearing an impossibly high fence. In that inner circuit of the mind and heart around which consciousness flows in the invisible daily dressage of identity, I keep on coming back to Boll, of course, and the knowledge of repeated failure has made the prospect of writing about him increasingly daunting. Now, at last, an image has come to hand that seems proof against the sense of inadequacy and trespass that made me abort so many beginnings embarked on before this one. Who would have guessed that the ritually eloquent gesture of strangers dead three thousand years would at last provide me with a talisman to steel my nerve, take up my pen, and leap?

Writing about the difficulty of writing about Boll could become just another fudging of the jump. Let me say about it only this: where the subject lies close-quartered with the heart, getting words to work is hard. Such proximity makes them prey to so many meltdowns—into cliché, melodrama, exaggeration, pathos, sentimentality—that it's tempting to lapse into silence and say nothing, or rest content with the roughest of approximations. By contrast, in those more outlying orbits, occupied by topics remote from what moves us, prose can be cool, precise, rock-steady, durable. Go far enough from the bright sun of our feelings and there is so little emotional gravity that the weightlessness of objectivity can take over and allow all sorts of verbal acrobatics to be performed with ease. Boll occupies my planet's core, so any words I use about him have to be cast to withstand the temperatures and pressures that govern there. I'm not sure if this is possible. They may end up being warped and twisted into shapes that can no longer carry the cargo I so much want them to bear.

Apart from the general difficulties that attend the chronicling of any intimacy, I have held off writing about Boll for two additional reasons. First, the knowledge that anything I write will, inevitably, seem like my memorial to him. Since any memorial is necessarily inadequate, efforts to erect one are rendered futile from the start. Secondly, there is a sense that, if anything is said, it should be said in a key in which I find it hard to pitch my voice. Boll's life seems to call for the delicacy of touch of a poem rather than an essay's weight of words. The clumsiness of gathered sentences seems almost an affront, risking something close to desecration.

These difficulties notwithstanding, I find myself back in the same ancient Scottish town where he died five years ago, watching the seagulls wheel and cry like lost and dissonant pieces of some urgent, broken utterance, as the dawn breaks into morning, slowly splitting the dark with its unstoppable wedges of light. I sit at a desk by a high window and search for words that might hold some sense of the preciousness of Boll's being and the loss his passing caused. Armed with my new, unbidden talisman, discovered quite by accident, I feel able, as I have not felt able before, to attempt the jump of writing about my son's brief existence and its impact on my own.

II

Like any talisman, the potency of this one is not self-evident. In revealing it I'm aware of how easily what is sacred in one context can appear mundane, even ridiculous, in another. I'm reminded of the anthropologist Colin Turnbull's experiences with the Ituri Pygmies. In his book *The Forest People*, Turnbull describes the key role played in the Pygmies' religious life by the *molimo*, or sacred trumpet. It is used by the tribe's elders to "waken the forest," on whose complex webs of life the Pygmies are utterly dependent. Eventually, having gained their trust, Turnbull is shown the molimo, which is treated with great reverence and secrecy. To his surprise, the Pygmies' most sacred object turns out to be a length of metal drainpipe.

The image that has allowed me to write about Boll acts like a kind of molimo, allowing me to waken the past and summon back from there the delicate web of a life that's gone. But I know that, to other eyes, my molimo may appear as ill-fitted to its task as a length of metal drainpipe does for anything sacramental.

Where the Ituri Pygmies found their molimo, I don't know. Mine was discovered in the Ulster Museum in Belfast, when I was looking round the *Early Ireland* exhibition. On a display board headed "Ideas and Beliefs," I read that no evidence survives of the ideas, feelings, and customs of Ireland's Mesolithic people. Then, in the same section, showing how such inner invisibilities may be inferred, even though they leave behind no direct residue of their nature, there was a simple black and white drawing of a burial. The caption beside it said:

> In a grave at Vedbaek, Denmark, archaeologists discovered the remains of a young woman buried alongside an infant lying on a swan's wing.

I had no swan's wing for Boll. Compared to the wordless eloquence with which these ancient Danes laid their treasured infant to rest, what I did for mine seemed clumsy and inarticulate. But though I admire the elegant simplicity of their gesture—its assured and accurate statement of feeling, the high level of symbolic competence it showed, the fact that they knew exactly what to do — I know I should not envy it. Such fluency with loss could come only with practice. We are not used to infant death.

III

In his Wilde lectures on comparative religion, delivered at the University of Oxford in 1972, John Bowker presents a picture of religion as an attempt to plot a meaningful way through the impenetrable and frightening limitations with which our lives are hedged. The unforeseeable nature of the future, the unreachable presence of the past, always at our heels, forever unalterable, no matter how much we might ache with regret and want to change what happened, the randomness of suffering, the fact of death — such things Bowker presents as limitations that threaten to circumscribe our existence and rob it of any sense of sense. The most threatening and intransigent of all limitations, says Bowker, is that of death. Religions attempt to forge a way through it by means of rituals that are sufficiently rich in symbolic associations that meaning seems assured. So, for example, burying a body "gains suggestive confirmation from the burial of a seed and the growth of a new plant." Or, tapping into a different key of association, burning a body "gains suggestive confirmation from the observation that burning anything releases something into the air, and leaves only a changed and much smaller part of whatever was there in the ashes." In the same way, floating a body out to sea "gains confirmation from the observation that salt dissolves in water." Bowker proposes that religions should be thought of as "route-finding activities, mapping the paths along which human beings can trace their way from birth to death and through death."

I have considerable doubt about the extent to which religions can offer any kind of reliable route through life, still less that they can somehow liberate us from the "limitations" Bowker identifies. Indeed such limitations might better be seen simply as conditions of life rather than constraints; they are things that define as much as threaten us. Does it make any more sense to say that we need to find a "way through" the "limitation" of oxygen dependency than it does to say that we need to find a way through death? Breathing and mortality are fundamental characteristics of our existence, not unnatural hurdles that stand in the way of its fulfillment and have somehow to be overcome. This (serious) criticism apart, I think Bowker does put his finger accurately on an important part of the consolation religions offer in the face of things that are hard to bear, via their recourse to well-chosen symbols.

Certainly the resonance suggested by my unexpected Ulster Museum talisman is consoling. The silent symbolic notes that are sounded in the heart by the gesture of laying a dead infant on a swan's wing and placing it thus cushioned in the grave play gently over a range of comforting tones with unobtrusive virtuosity. The whiteness and purity of a swan's virginally regal plumage deftly catch something of the unsullied nature of the small life borne upon it and of the fact that its newness and fleetingness made it all the more valuable, as priceless as a prince or princess of the rarest and most royal blood. The softness of feathers makes them a fitting cradle for unhardened bones. The strength and vigour suggested by the fact that they came from a swan-sized and swan-natured bird is a reminder of iron-in-the-softness: the fact that we would defend our children to the death. At home in water and in air, elements that boast a freedom not so obviously manifested in the earth, a swan's wing suggests the possibility of movement and escape. And, above all else, the wing suggests *flight*, an arising into the sky, a shaking off of heavy corporeal shackles, an unfettered soaring of the spirit. Freedom. Life.

What I'm presenting here as ritual competence may seem no more than superstition, ignorance, wishful thinking. I know (and have no doubt that the grieving adults of Vedbaek knew this too) that no swan's wing has the power to raise even the tiniest, lightest corpse from the irreversible gravity of death. The burial at Vedbaek displays symbolic eloquence, not failed magic. It became my talisman not because it offered some incredible "way through" the fact of death by escaping from or denying it, but because it chose to frame that fact in a particular way. It is a way that uses the razor's edge of our mortality to incise a boundary of high value around the life of a child, rather than sever the jugular of sense with the knowledge of our common annihilation.

Effective though it has been in facing a sense of loss that at times felt as though it might overwhelm me completely, I'm glad to have discovered my talisman only years after Boll's death. If I'd realized at the time how fitting a gesture it was, I'd have been faced with the awkward issue of where to find a swan and how to kill it. Indeed this would have been a legal as well as a practical conundrum since swans are considered "royal birds" in the UK and it's an offence to kill one. As it was, shocked by his death and inarticulate with grief, I fell back on more recent and socially sanctioned traditions of coping with the "limitation" of death—a small white coffin, black hearse, prayers offered to a god I don't believe in by a minister of a church to which I don't belong.

IV

"Boll" was the name chosen by Lucy, my then-three-year-old daughter. She was keen to find something that would fit a boy or girl since we didn't know, and didn't wish to discover until the moment of birth, what gender our second child would be. I don't know whether she'd heard "Boll" somewhere, or made it up, or if it was a variation on "ball" (though the pronunciation was subtly different). Leaning her head against Jane's swelling belly as the pregnancy progressed, she would sometimes talk to Boll, tell him/her what the world was like and that she too had once occupied "mummy's tummy." When Boll started to kick, she was delighted at this sign of an imminent playmate and patted where she thought his hand might be. Boll was included in her bedtime ritual and bidden "night, night" along with us. Things progressed without any indication of the imminence of tragedy. Everything seemed "normal." All the usual checks yielded all the usual results. We went to some antenatal classes, though without the same earnestness as first time round. As full term approached, we visited the labour suite of the hospital so it would be familiar territory on the day. Jane bloomed and swelled. Boll's movements grew more vigorous. You could see the live pulse of soon-to-be independent life in a growing repertoire of movements that momentarily—magically—dented and rippled his mother's flesh.

One afternoon only two weeks before his due date, Jane felt an unaccustomed stillness and the absence of anyone inside her. It was as if his familiar presence had suddenly and inexplicably gone away. The local doctor failed to find a heartbeat. He tried to offer comfort, assuring us that this sometimes happens and doesn't necessarily mean anything more than that the baby's position has rendered the heart temporarily inaudible. But at the hospital he was soon pronounced dead. Jane was induced. We went through the long hours of labour still hoping against hope. After all, doctors can be wrong. On this occasion, though, they'd made no mistake. When at last he was born, Boll turned out to be a beautiful, but lifeless, boy.

I don't want to say much more about the birth itself. It's not that I've forgotten—in fact I remember its unfolding with complete clarity— it's just that some things seem improper to disclose, seem to warrant discretion, not description. They demand privacy with the same silent authority by which the dead bid us shut their eyes and draw some veil across their face. Later, the hospital told us that it used to be the custom in cases of stillbirth for the infant's body to be spirited away immediately, as if the whole thing had never happened. No one was allowed to see, still less touch or hold it. We were at least fortunate to suffer our loss at a period of medical thinking that saw the wisdom in letting parents nurse the warm body of their child in an unhurried manner, only surrendering it when they felt ready to do so. So, obeying the deep-rooted instinct to rock a child in your arms, on your knee, we rocked our beautiful Boll, and his terrible unresponsive stillness and silence, his eventual unwarmable coldness, led to a surer acceptance of what had happened than if he'd been taken from us and hidden away.

No one was ever able to tell us, then or later, why he died. He was perfect in every respect save that he came into the world with a heart that had stopped beating and with lungs that would never take a breath. There were tests, there was an autopsy. We met with all the specialists. But his death remained a mystery; it would not yield up the secret of its untimely occurrence to any expertise. There seemed to be no reason for it. It was just one of those hard facts of life that hurts a lot and never goes away. It demands endurance; it does not admit of any cure.

V

A key question for many people was whether Boll had been born alive and then died, or been born dead. This (to me Jesuitical) distinction seemed to demarcate two quite different categories of response. According to which applied, our loss was viewed as serious or merely unfortunate. For those who asked this question, a stillbirth was seen as far less traumatic, almost as if it didn't count. In their view it meant that Boll had never really been. As such, we'd not lost anyone and so it simply didn't matter much, certainly not on the same scale as it would have done if, say, he'd drawn breath and lived for—well, I'm not sure how long would have been needed for him to have qualified for membership in the other constituency of loss: a few minutes, an hour, days, weeks, years?

This view, never expressed in so many words but clearly evident from some people's attitude, saw Boll as an incipient person only, someone (in fact, not quite someone) who had never managed to arrive in the company of other people. He was seen as not quite human, so not deserving of full-scale grief. Since the earth had never borne the independent weight of his tread, since he had not made any noises audible beyond the womb, since he had never drawn breath or felt the sun fall directly on his face, they reasoned that he had never really been here properly, in fact, that he had never really *been* at all and that, consequently, his not-being too was suspect, different, inferior, second class, something that could not cause bereavement in the same way as someone born alive. To those who reasoned thus, our loss of Boll belonged in the same grey area of pain, rarely spoken of, almost illicit, that accompanies miscarriage and termination.

I know how difficult it is to determine when a person begins and when he or she ends and so adjudge the rights and wrongs of abortion or euthanasia. These are areas of contention into which I have no wish to enter here. But I know I held a person in my arms, a someone, not a something, albeit snuffed out before we could ever look into each other's eyes. I'm as certain that Boll didn't cease to be a person simply because his fingers never tightened in a grip around my thumb as I'm sure that my father ceased to be himself long before he died. To my surprise, I shed many more tears for Boll than for him. Dad's death came after a long, full life and when illness had so eroded his health that continuance in the end was cruel; Boll's death was in every way the opposite of opportune or welcome. Physically, Boll was perfect, complete, fully formed, no different in appearance from any other newborn infant — except that his heartbeat and movement, so vigorous behind his mother's curtaining of flesh, had slipped secretly into stillness in the sepulchre of the womb.

In his poem "In Memory of Angelica," Jorge Luis Borges talks about "[h]ow many possible lives must have gone out in this so modest and diminutive death." Contrasting it with his own eventual extinction, at which "a certain past would die," when his six-year-old niece drowned in a swimming pool it was as if "a yet-to-be" had died. This catches something of the desolation felt at Boll's death, a desolation that had a different, more desperate flavour to it than anything my father's dying caused. Partly I think this had to do with the sense of lost potential, of something struck down, taken away before it could unfold, a story left unfinished just as it was starting. In part it also had to do with an absence of those tokens of familiar presence by which, with most deaths, we can pace our sense of loss and bereavement. For years after his death I wore my father's shirts, sat in the chairs he used to sit in, read the books that still bore his name signed strongly on the flyleaf. With Boll there was nothing to ease his going, no traces that might have gentled the sense of annihilation, made it more acceptable through the illusion of seeming to be gradual. He was gone with a suddenness and finality that was hard to bear. His was, to use Borges's words again, "a white future blindly obliterated by the stars." The nothingness he left was, is, stunning.

VI

I'm not sure if it's another ripple of symbolism emanating from my swan's-wing talisman, or if it's something I would have done anyway, but when I visit my son's grave now I often take a feather and leave it there, quill pushed into the earth as if it's a flower-stalk. I know the wind will blow it away before long, and I know it can do nothing in any practical sense. It cannot effect any change in what has happened; it can offer Boll no comfort since, however much I may wish to comfort him, I know he is not there. He is lost even to the most extravagant expression of longing, let alone to this bringing of flotsam. This is another gesture of the heart, not the head. Feathers, like seashells (I bring them, too), seem almost like tokens of long life because of their close association with the creatures that bore them and their continuance in a semblance powerfully reminiscent of the appearance of the living body. I do not set out to look for things to bring, but bring things come across by chance as I've been walking, whether by the sea or in the mountains or the woods. Offering such everyday souvenirs is the closest I can come to sharing walks with Boll. And for the same reason of impossible companionship I sometimes take a stone from his grave and carry it in my pocket for a while, where it warms with my body's heat and then cools as soon as I put it down again. At one level I know such actions make no sense, or that what little sense they do make is of an unwelcome variety, skirting, if not entering, realms of which I would rather not claim citizenship—the superstitious, the sentimental, the mawkish. Is it possible to find consolation without conning oneself into making almost sacramental a loss whose true index of value admits of nothing positive, whose raw unpalatable taste is that of an open grave and a small cold body and the knowledge that no communion of meaning can summon back what has gone forever?

Thinking about death and feathers brings to mind the ancient Egyptian belief that the judgment we face after death involves weighing the deceased's heart against *Maat*. Maat, sometimes pictured as a goddess, though more often thought of in abstract terms, as a concept rather than a deity, has to do with truth, order, justice, regularity, the maintenance of things according to their accepted patterns. The earthly duty of the pharaohs was to uphold Maat, indeed to be its embodiment and representative, royal bastions against chaos. The Egyptians believed that when we die, our hearts are placed on one side of a set of scales and Maat's symbol, a feather, is placed on the other. We are brought to account according to how well we fitted in with life's essential pattern: how much we challenged the natural order, the way things ought to be. Looking at the various pictures of this scene, as it is depicted in the *Egyptian Book of the Dead*, prompts a mix of emotions. Aesthetically, I've always found myself drawn to the ancient Egyptian style. There's a simplicity of line and colour I find pleasing, a clarity and straightforwardness—almost boldness—in the ready celebration of sensuality and beauty. At some other level, the animal-headed deities address a less explicable attraction. The Ibis-headed Thoth, Anubis's chilling jackal features, Horus's hawk's head, seem to people dramas with whose intricate and complex unfoldings I have long been familiar, but not at any level over which consciousness can claim suzerainty. Are they the stuff of dreams, perhaps, so that seeing them depicted prompts memories of the forgotten script of sleep? Or do they touch that potent human nerve that snakes its way mysteriously throughout our history, making us raise up symbols to put faces on our terrors and desires?

As with death's removal of anyone loved, I often wonder if there is any part of Boll that might have survived his seeming annihilation. The picture-book eschatology of the Egyptian papyri suggests a richly imagined post-mortem existence. For example, in one of the illustrations in the *Papyrus of Hunefer* (which dates from around 1370 BC), Anubis is shown leading the deceased Hunefer by the hand into the hall of Maat, where his heart is being weighed on a gigantic pair of scales. Thoth watches and records the result, while a maned, green-headed creature midway between dog and lion, mouth slightly open to reveal its fangs, sits and watches. This is Ammit, "Eater of the Dead." Part of the ritual of weighing the essence of the person, his heart, his conscience, the sum total of his earthly deeds distilled into a soul or spirit, involved the "Protestation of Innocence." This is where the deceased addresses each of the gods in turn. Each deity is assured that the speaker did not commit a particular sin, that he cannot be arraigned for disturbing the balance of Maat, for disrupting the order of things, for muddying truth or thwarting justice.

It strikes me that it is only the unborn or the very young who could offer up a Protestation of Innocence that would be truly credible. This sense of being wholly blameless increases the feeling of injustice at Boll's death, the sense that Maat was flouted by so premature an end. It also provides some slight measure of fugitive reassurance. For if there *is* any judgment of the dead, there would, surely, be no grounds on which he could be sentenced. The grim figure of Ammit is a nightmare for parents. A child dying passes forever beyond their protection; they can only hope there are no monsters in any world beyond as there are in this one. Or, if there are, that there might also be guardians who would be moved by the lonely innocence of a child's vulnerable spirit and stand guard beside its unaccompanied presence, protecting it from harm. I'm reminded, often, of Louis MacNeice's poem "Prayer Before Birth," which surely expresses the hopes and fears not of the unborn who apparently speaks the verses but of the parents. MacNeice lists "the blood-sucking bat," "the club-footed ghoul," "the man who is beast or who thinks he is God" among those that might threaten to harm this imagined imminent life, who asks for

> . . . water to dandle me, grass to grow for me, trees to talk
> to me, sky to sing to me, birds and a white light
> in the back of the mind to guide me.†

I wished all this and more for my son. But the white light in the back of his mind was only the endless tundra of extinction, which I hope at least extends the mercy of being unpeopled by any of the demons MacNeice imagines.

Mostly, though, I put all imaginings of continuance from my mind. Except for odd moments, they are eclipsed by a certainty that death unravels us completely. Our thread may be re-spun into other forms at the level of the atoms and elements that for a time constitute our flesh, bones, feathers, shells; but our sense of self, what makes us who we are, that daily dressage of consciousness, is gone forever. Perhaps, in recognition of that fell fact, we should have had Boll cremated, since there is nothing tangible left at all when one so young is committed to the flames. We were gently warned that they would have consumed him completely. So we opted for burial instead, the weight of the tiny coffin bearing the lie that there was something, someone still there. It was too difficult at the moment of bereavement to face parting from him completely, to contemplate vaporizing the tiny corporeal residue that was all we had left. But though burial might mask such complete absence in the immediate painful present, the process of unravelling conducted in the dark, in what in Scotland they call a lair (as if, like animals, we finally return to some familiar fastness to lick our wound of mortality), is as sure as fire. The bacteria and worms and beetles, the tiny microbes, the crushing pressure of the earth tumbled in on top of that frail pod, will do annihilation's work as surely as any furnace, only more slowly.

VII

At the end of December 2003, as I was drafting some ideas toward what would eventually become this essay, news was coming in of the earthquake that devastated the historic Iranian city of Bam. It left many thousands dead. I know that on any Richter scale of suffering, Boll's passing would scarcely register a tremor. What is a single, silent ceasing-to-be, one tiny life eclipsed within the gentle enclosure of its mother's body, compared to acres of visible devastation and entire families violently snuffed out? One of the images that has stayed in mind from the scores of terrible photographs generated by this cataclysm is of a father carrying his two sons to their grave. They are maybe four and six. The picture is a rear view, so we are spared looking at the face of someone visited by such grief. The father cradles a boy in each arm, held tightly against him, their bruised lifeless faces visible over his shoulders, their arms hanging loosely by his side. In the midst of so much death he was denied even the small comfort of laying them to rest in a chosen grave. Instead, the sheer scale of what happened meant communal burial, trenches full of bodies, the dead laid side by side in anonymous rows and earth hurriedly bulldozed over them.

Comparison of pain can quickly become grotesque, if not odious. There is no way we can accurately compute the weights that suffering's many guises variously lay upon us. Did the grieving parents of the child at Vedbaek or the father carrying his dead children at Bam feel more sorrow? Is the widow bereaved after fifty years of happy marriage more afflicted with grief than the mother who loses a baby before it draws its first breath? Does a deeper sense of anguish attend those lost to earthquake, flood, volcano, or those slaughtered in some genocidal frenzy? Should we delight more in the rescue from the rubble of Bam of a six-month-old baby or an eighty-year-old woman? To pose such questions with any expectation that they can be answered would be obtuse. What arithmetic of loss we can work out is simple, brutal, shocking in love's ruthless partiality. I have no doubt that the father at Bam, the parents at

Vedbaek, the parents of Boll would have sacrificed one another's children if that could have saved their own; that they would have consigned untold numbers of strangers to the grave as readily as any Nero if it could have kept their own flesh and blood cradled in life's swan's wing for just a little longer, cushioned against the dark of death.

History's holocaust threatens to dwarf any individual extinction into insignificance. Of what importance is any particular loss when set beside the fact that everything that has ever been alive, that is alive, that will ever be alive will also perish? Boll's momentary being, the secret hidden intimacies of his conception and development, the silent moment of his death, these are such very little things when put against the backdrop of what there is. They can seem reduced to complete unimportance simply by placing the weight of comparison alongside them. All those huddled corpses in the snow at Stalingrad, the thousands killed in the Battle of the Somme, the ash-covered corpses at Pompeii, mass graves at Treblinka, rivers flowing with bloated, butchered bodies in Rwanda—such things can make my tears for Boll seem ridiculous, self-indulgent, out of all proportion to the enormity of loss that others suffer. In *Escape from the Anthill*, Hubert Butler notes the way in which we are now assailed by intrusive information about the experiences of strangers in places remote from us. Facts "settle like butterflies on the brain till every cell is clogged with the larvae from their unwanted eggs." Butler asks how we can protect ourselves "from the ravages of secondhand experience." Such ravages can easily end up pulverizing individual anguish into irrelevance by making it seem grotesquely disproportionate. Yet for all the terrible dwarfing that history's dire colossi of pain can effect, throwing their huge shadows across our lives and eclipsing anything Boll-scaled, the only power such colossi have in the end is that they too are rooted in individual anguish.

VIII

Those who attended Boll's birth were beyond reproach in their conduct. The midwives in particular (whose tears enhanced rather than dented their professionalism) handled what was a difficult situation for everyone with enormous competence and care. Some while afterward, though, an anonymous "health-care professional," of whose role I am uncertain, advised—in answer to a question about how Boll's death might affect his three-year-old sister—that at that age "they" are very resilient and that she'd forget all about it in two or three weeks. With the assessment of resilience I concur; as for forgetting, this was entirely wide of the mark. We have been careful neither to emphasize nor ignore what happened, but to treat it as honestly and openly as possible. In our judgment, it was inappropriate for a three-year-old to see her baby brother's body or to attend the funeral, though later she has accompanied us (as, more recently, has her younger sister) on our infrequent visits to the grave—infrequent not through any choice, but because we were living only temporarily in Scotland when Boll died there and are domiciled hundreds of miles from where our son is laid to rest. Five years later Lucy still talks about the brother she almost had. And she wishes we had let her see him.

In part, I suspect that the experience of Boll's death was profoundly different for the three of us, in part the same. For Jane, who had been so intimately conjoined to her son for nine months, who had each day felt his emergent life growing within her, his death honed the blade of loss to a keenness it is hard for my blunter male perspective to appreciate. I know it cut her more deeply than anything had done before. For Lucy, at three, struggling to make sense of the finality of death, her brother's dis-appearance posed a problem of an order of difficulty that adults schooled in loss can scarcely grasp. She moved from the ludicrous (why didn't we just put Boll in a glass case and fit him with batteries?) to the assured realization of what loss really means with a speed that was impressive. All of us intermittently ask ourselves, and sometimes one another, what would have happened if he had lived, what Boll would be like now, what sort of person our unmet son or brother would have been. Often we feel his shadow when we see a child of comparable age. And, with the birth of Laura, our second daughter, two years after Boll died, the slightness of the chance that any of us exist was emphasized. For, if he had lived, she would almost certainly never have come to be. Her existence is the unexpected blessing bestowed by his extinction. Though we could not have thought it at the time, seen in the light of this new life the desolation of our bereavement was not to be the wholly barren, bitter fruit it seemed.

Things that show what is no longer there exert a special fascination. For instance, there is a poignancy about tracks in sand or snow when no one is in sight. But photographs are perhaps our most potent and familiar amber, through which we can gaze at the denizens of the recent past, trapped in their smiling poses as surely as any prehistoric insect caught and preserved in pine resin. I have one photograph of Jane, heavily pregnant with Boll, standing in the tropical ravine in Belfast's Botanical Gardens, only a stone's throw from the museum with the then-undiscovered talisman of the swan's-wing burial at Vedbaek. In the amber of that moment Boll was alive. We were animated with expectation. Now, whenever we pause and smile to the camera, he is not there, and still he is not there and never will be with us. So every family photo now contains the invisible ghost of his absence. And I know we are forever diminished by his loss, no matter how softly I try to lay his memory upon a swan's wing of words.

For how long should we remember the dead? I have no answer. Sometimes I almost forget, then something happens to make it all come flooding back with a sharpness that makes me doubt the power of time to erode into bluntness the sharp edges of this particular death. Last summer robins nested in a shed in our garden. Watching them gather moss and twigs to build the nest, I suggested to Lucy she might like to help. So we stripped the hair out of her hairbrush and left it in a flower-bed where the robins often hopped about. They bred successfully and raised a brood. For a time, before the territorial imperative made them disperse, we were able to watch the whole family, red-breasted adults energetically collecting food for their spotty, still clumsy juveniles. In the winter, we removed the nest (they build them new each season).

In it, there was one unhatched egg and, wound about the shallow cup, clearly visible, strands of human hair. Boll left not even a single hair in the world that a robin might gather for its nest. There is nothing anywhere that is his. But we felt him, still feel him, in our midst, as certainly as a brooding bird must feel an egg beneath her.

Perhaps the Vedbaek burial on a swan's wing was the precursor of a trend that later characterized some of the contents of cremation urns found elsewhere in Denmark. Along with the ashes in these Bronze Age artifacts, archaeologists have found the wings of jackdaws, crows, and rooks. As Hilda Davidson puts it in her book *Pagan Scandinavia*, the presence of birds' wings emphasizes "the idea of a journeying spirit." I often wonder where Boll's journey has led him, whether to the full stop of annihilation or, somehow, to another destination. But such speculations are, I fear, merely the stuff of desperation, wishful thinking, rooted in the barren soil of impossibility. For where would there be room for all our wandering spirits, for all the deaths that have happened across time such that sometimes the planet itself seems not unlike a giant catafalque hurtling through space, densely laden with our remains? The anonymous ashes dusting jackdaws' wing-feathers, the pharaohs in their sarcophagi, the nameless slaves entombed with them, the cindered remains of the war-slaughtered, the bodies laid out in neat composure in well-ordered cemeteries, the pits for the plague-stricken, the bones that gently move to the rhythm of the tides as the sea erodes them back into their elements, the crushed and asphyxiated thousands of Bam. It is no wonder that as we weave our way among the remains we are soon fated to join, we, the temporarily living, grasp at straws, look for ways through death's defining limitation, seek out any swan's wing of comfort that might gentle our hard way for us.

Before I die and my ashes join Boll in his cold lair, I want to take a blackbird's feather from the County Antrim garden where so much of my childhood was spent. I will bear it carefully across the sea to Scotland and, at some quiet time when there will be no witnesses to such groundless shamanism, I will push it into the earth beside my son's headstone. I will quietly say some words, hope to feel the shiver of some sense of a presence I know cannot be there. Then I will go again, leaving the feather to conduct into the dark earth in which he lies a tiny ripple of vibration, as if from a wind-stirred tuning fork, a natural prayer flag, bearing with its movement the memory of flight and song chirruping out of a bright yellow beak to greet the morning as the light comes, gently illuminating the world from which he is long vanished, leaving us to try to cope as best we can—with words, with images, with imaginings and secret rituals stolen from other times and other places. Knowing all the while that what we have to cope with is as resistant to our wish that it were otherwise as granite is to the whisper of our pleading breath upon it.

CHRIS ARTHUR is author of five essay collections, most recently *On the Shoreline of Knowledge* (Iowa/Sightline, 2012). A new and selected essays volume, *Words of the Grey Wind*, appeared in 2009. His work has been published in a range of journals, including *The American Scholar*, *Irish Pages*, *Northwest Review*, *Orion*, *Southern Humanities Review*, *Southwest Review*, and *The Threepenny Review*. A member of Irish PEN, he has been the recipient of a number of literary awards. These include the Akegarasu Haya International Essay Prize, the Theodore Christian Hoepfner Award, and the Gandhi Foundation's Rodney Aitchtey Memorial Essay Prize. His work has been included in *Best American Essays* (and also mentioned half a dozen times in the Notable Essays lists of this annual series). Further information about his writing can be found at chrisarthur.org. Chris Arthur lives in St. Andrews, Scotland.

†Louis MacNeice, "Prayer Before Birth," *Collected Poems*, ed. E.R. Dodds (London: Faber and Faber, 1966).

Loving Benjamin

GAIL MARLENE SCHWARTZ

PART FIVE: BEGINNING
His eyes are dark and warm, like hot chocolate, and his movements are punctuated and full of life, like a baby Charlie Chaplin. His new lips feel strangely capable on my nipple.

His gaze meets mine and I whisper, "Well hello, Benjamin," my voice grainy from the surgery.

I nurse him hello and I nurse him goodbye. I haven't seen him since.

PART ONE: ANOTHER BEGINNING
"Congratulations!"

I listen to the message three times to make sure it's real. Finally, I drop the phone and bolt out the door, barefooted, running to find Lucie who is walking the dog, shouting, "We're pregnant! We're pregnant!!!"

PART TWO: WAITING AND WEIGHING
Our first ultrasound happens at eight weeks. The tech rubs jelly on my belly and a tiny pulsing heart appears on the screen.

And then, another.

Two bodies. Two heartbeats.

At home that evening, we celebrate with flowers, two yellow mums for them, a white for Lucie and a purple for me. We light candles, hold hands, and weep with joy.

I step on the scale. 161. No gain yet.

Our doctor gives me screening tests at week twelve. Afterwards she sits us down; she's concerned about the nuchal translucency test, which indicates that Baby B has a one in three chance of having Down syndrome. She strongly recommends an early amniocentesis, which would be definitive: "I could do it tomorrow," she says. Ninety-five percent of women who get this news choose abortion, she tells us, and if it's necessary, sooner is better for the healthy twin.

I am numb and cannot speak.

We finally take an appointment for the amniocentesis in a few days to give ourselves time to think. I cry silently in the car going home, wiping my cheeks and nose with the grey fleece of my jacket.

During the next few days, I think about my fantasy children. One girl and one boy. Talented and smart. Musician and cartoonist. Successful. People who other people cherish. People who care for the world and make me proud.

Of course, neither of these children has Down syndrome.

Retarded. Slow. Special needs. Mentally handicapped.

Somebody who ninety-five percent of people choose to abort.

No, this news does not fit into my plans at all.

Suddenly I am deeply ashamed. I want to tuck myself into the corner, under the loose floorboard in our bedroom, where nobody can see me.

Lucie and I talk for hours. We already feel like parents and realize that abortion is not an option for us. Our research tells us that Down syndrome babies are easily adoptable by families who feel called to raise special needs kids.

I step on the scale. Again and again and again.

165

165

168

My brain does somersaults around the one in three odds. Sixty-six percent of the people who get this news have normal kids, I reason.

Medical doctors are such alarmists. Two out of three, two out of three, two out of three.

I see a new mom pushing her twins in a double stroller down the street. I turn around and cover four extra blocks to avoid her.

171

172

174

We do it up for Halloween. We spend hours on our costumes, Lucie a witch and me, the Headless Horseman. We make an orange themed dinner for friends — sweet potato fries, pumpkin soup, and cheese puffs. We light candles and carve intricate designs into pumpkins with the help of Martha Stewart.

172

175

175

I feel my capacity for closeness shut down, like a trap door, and I sink deeper and deeper into the darkness. I stop returning phone calls and start going back to bed after breakfast. Sometimes I stay there until lunch.

I think of my own mother, just twenty-two at my birth. An unplanned pregnancy, I wasn't the child she had imagined either — the beautiful, feminine girl who would play quietly with dolls, do as she's told, and take good care of Mommy.

Daily life with her was terrifying.

What if she had given me up?

175

176

175

PART THREE: MOVING THROUGH THE MIDDLE

The doctor calls two weeks later with the results of the amnio. Baby B has Down syndrome.

The waiting is over.

I spend the day with Lucie. We cry and hold each other. We wander aimlessly around the house. I look for something to fill myself with: flax toast with peanut butter, semi-sweet chocolate morsels, Lucky Charms cereal with rice milk, a Granny Smith apple and some cheddar.

The gaping hole remains in the depths of my pregnant belly.

In the evening, I make the mistake of calling my mother. She listens silently for a moment before speaking. "You're not going to *keep* it, are you?" I hang up quietly and lie down on the couch and stay there, staring at the window, until morning.

We talk at breakfast before Lucie leaves for work. We know deep in our hearts that we cannot provide for Baby B. Our advancing ages and my career are reason enough.

The shame I feel about having a defective child can stay neatly tucked inside me. My heart can now rest, knowing that Baby B will be fully loved and accepted by his adoptive parents.

179

177

178

I float out, farther and farther from my tribe. I am too broken to manage others' reactions, judgments, even their clumsy kind offers of "can I do anything to help?"

179

180

180

I spend more and more time in bed.

PART FOUR: LOSING AND GAINING

Quietness. Emptiness. Agony.

My belly pushes out, more and more, and I sleep in short spurts. My maternity pants keep falling down and I can't walk to the corner without feeling breathless.

We find out that they are two boys and decide to name them: Baby A is Alexi, our son. Baby B is Benjamin. We use their hospital initials to honour their time as twins, kicking, elbowing, and hiccupping inside me.

182

183

184

Between weeks thirty-two and thirty-three, the adoption proceedings begin: we shed tears of relief to find out there is a family waiting for little Benjamin.

Repeated questions about us being sure of our decision are difficult. We are sure . . . and we are sad.

185

187

187

Occasionally I am still overtaken by fear. "What's wrong with the other one?" "What if something happens at the birth?" "What if I am a terrible mother?"

I feel kicks and see elbows and heels glide across my middle so I focus there. The fear retreats into the shadow of the miracle and starts losing its grip on me.

190

191

192

PART FIVE: BEGINNING, AGAIN

At thirty-six weeks, my doctor tells me I am having light contractions and that Benjamin's heart rate is dropping dangerously low with each one. She suggests going ahead with an induction, knowing how important a vaginal birth is to me. "We can always wheel you across the hall to the OR for a C-section if there's any problem." I look at her, puzzled. "But couldn't Benjamin die quickly with stronger contractions?" She just looks at me, and finally shrugs. I realize then that my doctor is thinking only of Alexi. She is willing to sacrifice Benjamin, seeing him like most of the outside world will see him. My mind runs through all of the reasons C-sections are bad for babies; this is not how I want my son to enter the world. But at that moment, I am Benjamin's mother too, his birth mother, and my job at that moment is clear. I make the decision and the nurses begin prepping me for surgery.

I tell our doula, Leslie, and the hospital staff that I do not want to see Benjamin at all after the birth; I need to focus on Alexi and not get bogged down in grief.

Frightened and shivering, I am wheeled into the OR in my gown. I am given several medications in my spine and slowly sensations in my bottom half fade away. Lucie comes in after about fifteen minutes and holds my hand. At some points I am losing so much blood that I am certain I'll vomit. Finally they pull Alexi out and I hear him wail. The nurse puts him on my chest for a few moments before whisking him away to be cleaned. They take Benjamin out next and quickly bring him elsewhere.

When we arrive in the recovery room, both babies are there: it seems the doctors had forgotten my request. A nurse takes Alexi away for some extra oxygen and Benjamin remains in his little plastic bassinet, quietly smacking his tiny lips together. Leslie comments casually that he wants to nurse. I throw caution to the wind, take him in my arms, and give it my best effort: my first moment of breastfeeding. He latches on and nurses like a pro, all the while maintaining eye contact.

His eyes are dark and warm, like hot chocolate, and his movements are punctuated and full of life, like a baby Charlie Chaplin. His new lips feel strangely capable on my nipple.

His gaze meets mine and I whisper, "Well hello, Benjamin," my voice grainy from the surgery.

I nurse him hello and I nurse him goodbye. I haven't seen him since.

GAIL MARLENE SCHWARTZ is a writer and performer living in Montreal. Recent publications include "Pack the Car, Honey" (*GO Magazine*), "A Few Good Men" (*Gay Parent*), and most recently her play *Crazy: One Woman's Search for Sanity*, in the anthology *Hidden Lives*, published by Brindle & Glass. Check out her blog at twodykesandaboyby.blogspot.ca and her website at gailmarleneschwartz.weebly.com.

Story
ON THE ORDER OF THINGS OR WHAT I REALLY WANT TO SAY

JANET BAKER

FEBRUARY 17, 1960. AT the Winnipeg Women's Pavilion, my first pregnancy is full term and about to end. Labour has been induced. The nurse attaches electrodes to my stomach. I ask her why she's doing that. "The baby's going to die," I say. She's not listening. They're monitoring a baby who is going to die.

We've known for a week. The X-ray was ordered because it looked like a breech birth. The doctor's phone call comes shortly after I arrive home from my appointment.

"Can you and your husband come to my office in the morning?"

"Is it something to worry about?"

"Well, yes."

I phone my mother. She phones the doctor. "I didn't want to tell her over the phone," he says. "You're her mother, maybe you can tell her. The baby has a defect incompatible with life."

My husband and I go to his office the next morning. We're told the baby has anencephaly, a neural tube defect. We know nothing about neural tube defects. We only know our baby has an abnormality that is untreatable and fatal. The doctor says he prefers to wait a bit to see if nature will take its course.

I wait. The baby is still moving. I'm still in my maternity clothes. I'm waiting to give birth; the baby is going to die. A week later, I go to the hospital. They set up a Pitocin drip, wheel me into the operating room, break my water, wheel me out. Monitor. At the appropriate moment, I'm put to sleep.

I don't want to know if it was a boy or a girl, but after my husband has been called to sign the papers, I ask him. "It was a girl," he says. We don't know if she took a breath. I don't remember what we planned to name her. In those days, they kept mothers and babies about a week. I'm allowed to go home early. At my postnatal checkup the doctor advises that as soon as I feel up to it, we can try again.

ℒ   We get through it. A year later almost to the day I give birth to our daughter—full term, five and a half pounds, and perfect—unbelievably, miraculously ours. That beautiful moment, the day we take her home—there in the middle of that big hospital bed, just as she is about to be dressed and bundled to go, our baby sneezes. Her name is Lynn, her birthday February 19, 1961.

ℒ   March 1962. I'm four months pregnant, resting, because I've been having cramps. When my water breaks, I know it's over. I also know enough to save the evidence, so when I'm taken to the hospital for a D&C and they ask, I tell them "yes, I can get it here." I want to know if the fetus had a defect. They want to know what went wrong.

What goes wrong is that my mother and mother-in-law decide to get rid of the contents of that bucket I've left in the bathtub. The fetus I'd made sure to keep is flushed down the toilet along with any possible answers. They thought it best.

On February 16, 1963, as the doctor says, we have our pair. We name our son Garth. His middle name, Reed, has now been passed down through four generations of boys. We are truly blessed—a girl and a boy, two years apart, healthy.

In 1964, we move to Mississauga. We begin to think about having another child. I write to my obstetrician in Winnipeg. "In view of my history," I write, "should we just be happy with the two healthy children we have?" His reply is encouraging. In essence, "if you want another child, go for it." The first pregnancy was just one of those things, quite rare and unlikely to happen again; the miscarriage is something that happens to many women — not a reason to be concerned. I still have his letter in my dresser drawer. I should pull it out and put it with the family archives.

On March 19, 1966, our youngest son is born with myelomengocele, a neural tube defect. Our lives change forever.

He's born at 2:00 AM. I hold him on my tummy and breathe out nine months of apprehension: my baby is okay.

He's not okay, but I'm not told. My husband is not told.

My husband is shown the baby through the glass window of the nursery. It's the middle of the night, but that doesn't matter. Everyone's been waiting — the baby's overdue. Phone calls are made to Winnipeg. The word goes out: a boy, everything's fine.

I wake up early, euphoric but at the same time plagued by a lingering anxiety. I tell my roommate I won't really believe my baby's okay until I check him out for myself. The doctor appears at my bedside before breakfast. "The baby has a defect," he tells me, "it's serious but not insurmountable." I'm swimming in a dark pool that feels all too familiar. I try to take in what he is saying. "You were tired last night. I wanted you to sleep. I didn't tell your husband because he would have had to tell you. The baby needs surgery today, we'll need permission, they have to close the opening in his back, he may not have the use of his legs. There's the possibility of hydrocephalus, brain damage, kidney problems, incontinence. You can talk to the neurosurgeon."

I can't think but then I do think — of my other children — what effect will this have on my other children? — I remember saying those exact words. The doctor seems to reply that it can be good for them in some way. Everything is a blur. He leaves. I have to call my husband. It's been a long night. He's sleeping. My mother wakes him. She knows from my voice that something is very wrong.

Later the doctor asks my husband what the problem was with the first pregnancy. Forty-seven years ago, a different time—but in retrospect, unthinkable that he hadn't asked before, that it hadn't been discussed.

The baby is whisked to the Hospital for Sick Children. He survives the surgery. My husband goes to see him while I'm still in hospital, reassures me that he looks fine. I don't know what to expect, but a few days later, there I am and there he is—in an incubator, lying on his stomach on a special frame, his back covered with bandages, looking as peaceful and precious as any newborn. I don't remember if I was allowed to hold him. I do remember those first stirrings of hope, that unforgettable moment when a nurse asks, "What are you going to call him?"

"Gary," I tell her. "His name is Gary."

Twenty-seven years later, I do a painting of that baby, of Gary, stretched out on his tummy on his Bradford frame. In my mind, from the outset, this painting is called *His Name Is Gary*. I don't show it to anyone, not even my husband, for several months. I show it first to a trusted artist friend who says of my initial reluctance to show it, "It's from a time when your emotions were too raw." When I do show it I realize that what most people see is a baby with a smile, not a baby with a problem.

May 1966, the Sunday of the long weekend, Gary is still at Sick Kids. He now has a shunt for hydrocephalus, put in during his first week of life; he's had a couple of shunt revisions, has required more surgery on his back, has survived meningitis. We've been to Wasaga Beach for the day. The pictures are in our family album: Lynn and Garth wading in the water—two kids, a day at the beach. The phone call comes that night: Gary can come home. We are still hoping that he will have some use of his legs and that he hasn't suffered brain damage. What we do know is that we have to watch closely for signs of a blocked shunt. We also know Gary is a survivor.

How do I tell this story, the story of our family, of Gary, his twenty-nine years? Part of me wants to go digging through photograph albums, part of me resists, wanting to write from memory. Part of me is afraid to spend too much time looking at photograph albums, even though it has now been seventeen years since Gary died. Inexplicably, one photograph keeps coming into my head, a picture of Gary when he was about ten, sitting in his specially constructed hand-propelled bike. I know which album this picture is in, its multi-patterned cover. I know this album spent a lot of time with Gary during various extended stays in hospital. I know there is a picture of Gary holding a frog on one of our camping trips to Killbear Provincial Park—he was always up for a dare, no doubt the prime reason for this picture. But my mind keeps swinging back to Gary on his bike, back to that day, his grin, to the rest of us gathered around on the sidewalk in front of our house, Gary on his yellow bike, reflected in a puddle. I don't need to look at the picture. I choose memory.

🖋 I have to write this a little bit at a time, find my way. Where do I go from here? What I really want to say is that if I don't try, it will always be unfinished business. It is now midnight, though, and I should know better than to think about such things before bed.

🖋 Last night I dreamed I met Gary on the street, in downtown Toronto, near Sick Kids. In my dream, I haven't seen him for a long time. In my dream, I'd thought he was dead. At first, I don't recognize the young man in the power chair because he's sporting a long black wig. Then he comes closer and there is a sudden dizzying realization. I try to look for his trach scar, think I see it, but it isn't as prominent as I remember. I search his face. "Are you Gary?" "Yes," he says, but he looks past me, seems not to know me. He looks so well, so very well, so very independent. When I wake up, he's still with me. If he hadn't been wearing that ridiculous Tiny Tim wig, I could have seen the scars from his shunts. I think of the scars that covered his back—like a map of Europe, one of his seating consultants once said. If only I'd been able to see his back. Or the small scar on his arm, the scar that looked like it was from a cigarette burn. It happened in the hospital, a wound so deep it took several weeks to heal. Gary unable to enlighten us, we never knew what it was or how he got it. No one had an answer for us.

꙳ Growing up in Winnipeg, it was noted that I was "good at art." In Grade 3, I won a "Beautify Winnipeg" poster contest. I was encouraged and given private lessons, was art editor of the school yearbook for my three years of junior high. Then came high school, followed by an office job, marriage, and babies—no time for art.

In 1965, I decided it was time to make time. I bought the Time-Life Library of Art, vowing to work my way through all twenty-eight volumes. I enrolled in night courses at the Three Schools of Art in downtown Toronto, travelling by subway from Mississauga, first for life drawing, then oil painting. By the end of oil painting, I was nearing the end of my pregnancy with Gary. There would be no thoughts of art for ten years.

꙳ Here is where I must try to encapsulate what Gary's life was like, what our life was like with Gary. He became, of necessity, the centre of our existence.

As I ponder where to begin, I suddenly know where to begin—with the drawings his sister brought home, day after day, her entire kindergarten year. I still have them: drawings of our family, of Gary in his crib, the details of his room, drawings of him in a hospital room, the details of that room, an ambulance, sirens, the driveway of the hospital, our house, Gary, always surrounded by his family. Our family. Gary. Lynn was five years old when he was born, a little girl looking forward to playing little mother to her new baby brother—a little girl, with this baby brother, now having to come to terms with uncertainty as a daily given in her life, in his life, in our lives.

Uncertainty: the state of not knowing. We watch Gary's legs for any sign of movement—hoping maybe—but maybe those little twitches are just reflexive. We watch for signs of a blocked shunt, lethargy, vomiting. There are none. We begin to feel cautiously optimistic. During this, his first month at home, we fail to notice that his head is getting bigger. At his next appointment, the measurements tell the story. We see the neurosurgeon the next morning. There has probably been brain damage. He talks about options—surgery to prevent further damage or let the hydrocephalus progress, which probably means institutionalization. Gary is looking fine. There is only one option.

Shunt revisions become a recurring theme. The scars on Gary's back keep breaking down, requiring weeks of hospitalization and eventually major plastic surgery. I don't remember when he was first able to hold up his head while lying on his tummy, but I know it was a momentous achievement. I don't remember when he was first able to sit without being propped up with pillows. I do remember that we knew early on that he was going to have to get by without the use of his legs.

Life goes on. Like all parents, we take Gary along, wherever and whenever the older two are involved in their normal activities—at the pool, the hockey or lacrosse arena—or me at the curling rink. At first, it's no different than taking any child in a stroller, or holding any child on a lap. Eventually we acquire a stroller that will accommodate an adult. We are still mobile. He is growing, but I can still carry him upstairs to his bedroom and lift him into a car. The year his brother's hockey team wins the championship, they make a presentation to Gary, a Timex watch, engraved with his name just like all the other members of the team. They give him a special puck.

Gary spends extended periods of time at the Crippled Children's Centre in Toronto where they fit him, first for a flat platform on wheels, designed to hold him in a sitting position while providing mobility, then for a parapodium, a standing brace. Strapped in, from his chest down to the thick platforms under each foot, for the first time he is upright. Using a walker, he learns to swivel, but never masters the more effective swing-through gait. By now, he is in nursery school and something of a chatterbox, especially when it comes to stating his name.

I don't remember when Gary began to have seizures. What I remember vividly is the first one, the day I went to his room in the morning and found him in the grips of one. I had never seen a seizure. Gary's never stopped of their own accord—a seizure always meant a trip to the hospital, including one Christmas he spent in a hospital in Winnipeg, just a day after our arrival there for the holidays. Seizure medication was added to the mix, and it did work to a point, but the fear of a seizure was something we lived with on a daily basis.

I don't remember when Gary got his first wheelchair. I know it was before June 1978, when he was admitted to Sick Kids with a possible blocked shunt and didn't come home for a year. He spent six months in hospital, including several weeks in intensive care, followed by six months of rehab at the Crippled Children's Centre. That year, I spent an overnight at the hospital learning to manage his trach so that he could come home for Christmas. He got rid of his trach in the spring and came home in June, but was back in hospital a few months later—more complications, more time in intensive care. It would be another precarious six months before he came home again.

In 1984, we bought a wheelchair van and installed an elevator in our home. I remember that date, but I've lost track of most of the major surgeries and medical emergencies that are part of the story of our life with Gary. I had a list that I carried with me each time he was hospitalized or went to emergency. In those days, each sheet of paper came out of the printer attached to the previous sheet. I never tore them apart, just unrolled his record like a scroll when asked for his medical history. It simplified things.

We took Gary to New York, to Nashville, to Branson, Missouri, to Disney World. Before that, on family camping trips to Killbear, to Niagara, to the Maritimes, Winnipeg, Disney World campground. Gary loved music, especially country. We took him to shows at the CNE, Maple Leaf Gardens, other venues in Toronto. He was a fan of figure skating and curling. In 1991, we spent a week at the World Curling Championships, were in the stands at the Winnipeg Arena every day, Gary wearing his Canada sweater, cheering for the young Kevin Martin. We took Gary to skating shows, including the Canadian Championships in Hamilton in 1994 right after he got his feeding tube. Gary also loved *Wheel of Fortune*. One year, Pat and Vanna came to the CNE. When my name was drawn and I got to be on stage, Gary was my loudest supporter. I won my round, identifying Dustin Hoffman in short order. The other contestants didn't have a chance. I didn't just win my round. As a result of my win we were able to make contact with people who came through with three tickets to see *Wheel of Fortune* at Radio City Music Hall.

Gary was a huge fan of ten-pin bowling. A specially constructed ramp allowed him to propel the ball from his lap to the alley. His not-to-be missed Sunday morning league consisted of players with all types of disabilities, many of whom Gary had gone to school with and then more recently worked with in a sheltered setting. In May 1995, Gary's team captured the championship. Gary missed the last few weeks. At the banquet, a couple of weeks after his death, a Sportsmanship Trophy was unveiled in Gary's memory. Gary was the first recipient.

Gary died on May 11, 1995. He'd been on "borrowed time" since

November, but it could be said that this was the case for much of his life. He'd beaten the odds so many times we'd come to expect he would continue to do so. This time it wasn't to be. With a gastrostomy to facilitate feeding, he got an extra few months. They were good months. Gary loved Christmas. We wanted him to have Christmas. He got Christmas and his birthday.

✎ I had returned to painting in the late seventies. Gary loved to tell people I was an artist. Once, at his bedside in hospital, because I was so obviously versed in tending to his needs, someone asked if I was a nurse. On this topic, Gary was bent on being heard. "No! An artist!"

As a volunteer gatekeeper alongside my husband at our local Art in the Park event, Gary's job, stamping hands, gave him the opportunity to connect with people—absolutely one of his favourite pastimes. At art shows, Gary's responses to certain pieces often caught us by surprise. He seemed to look at artworks in the same way he looked at clouds, pointing out what he saw, making us look more closely. There were frequent drives in the country—the three of us, Gary and my husband in the parked van listening to favourite tapes, while I ran around photographing potential subject matter.

In 1993, I began to paint Gary. As the paintings grew in number, there was the sense that this was a series I needed to complete before it was too late. In 1994, I was invited to submit photos of my paintings of Gary and the story behind them to *American Artist* magazine. They responded that they'd like to do an article and would get back to me. Gary knew my paintings of him were to be in a magazine. In May 1995, the morning after his memorial service, the phone rang. It was the editor of *American Artist*, calling from New York, telling me that the article was going ahead and that they needed a picture of me, immediately. My husband happened to be going to New York just two days later. We took the photo in our backyard, and he was able to deliver it personally to the magazine's office, just a block away from his company's office. "Painting What Is Closest to Your Heart" appeared in the November 1995 issue of *Watercolour* magazine. One of the eight paintings showcased in this article was *His Name Is Gary*, the one of him as a baby. Gary loved the fact that I painted him but never commented on this painting. I'll never know whether he didn't see himself in it or whether he did and simply preferred not to.

꧁ I had been painting Gary for two years. I had no idea what direction my work would take when he died, but I found that I could still paint Gary from memory. Over time, I began to paint him from behind, Gary in his wheelchair, moving toward an imaginary, unidentifiable realm. Eventually, the paintings became just that realm.

My art has continued, through many stages. Gary's image is no longer in the work, but his presence is always in my work. In 2005, I took a giant leap of faith. Fifty-two years after graduating from high school, I enrolled as an undergraduate student in the Faculty of Fine Arts at the University of Victoria. Five years later, my husband, my son, and my daughter sat in the third row at my convocation. They greeted me afterwards with a bouquet of yellow roses. Gary's favourite colour was yellow. There we are in the picture, my husband, my son, and my daughter—and me holding yellow roses. The picture tells the story. In all our minds, Gary was there with us.

꧁ What I have related here is such a small part of the story. Gary enriched our lives in so many ways. The doctor was right when he responded to my question that first day of Gary's life, that it could only be good for my other children. It was good for all of us.

I realize now that the story of Gary will always be unfinished business. I can never tell it in its entirety. There will always be more to tell, unexpected memories waiting to be triggered. What I really want to say is that Gary is with us every day, in little things like bumping into a ceiling fixture or an over-the-top sneeze that would have cracked him up, or big things, like welcoming a new baby into the family. He is with us as we count the school buses lined up in the high school parking lot. He is with us every time we look at the moon, because Gary always stopped to look at the moon. What I really want to say is that if it had been possible to determine that the baby I miscarried had a neural tube defect, if it had been concluded that there was a high risk for future pregnancies, I don't know what direction our lives would have taken. We already had Lynn. Would I have had Garth? Would I have had Gary? Maybe my mother and mother-in-law, in their uninformed wisdom, got it right too.

JANET BAKER was born and grew up in Winnipeg. A practising artist for many years, she is an elected member of the Ontario Society of Artists and the Canadian Society of Painters in Watercolour. She and her husband have travelled widely, and continue to do so, but the purchase of a "retirement getaway" condo in Victoria in 2002 proved to be the springboard for the realization of a different dream: in 2010, as the result of a five-year hiatus from making art, Janet graduated from the University of Victoria with a Bachelor of Fine Arts degree. She juggles art and writing in Mississauga, Victoria, and elsewhere. Her first published poem appeared in the anthology *Walk Myself Home* (Caitlin Press, 2010).

How to Bury
a Yellow Toque

JESSICA HIEMSTRA

MY MOTHER INTRODUCED ME to swamp lanterns. We were walking somewhere near the University of British Columbia campus. She had embarked on her PHD. Dad had left her after twenty-three years of marriage. He put the canoe on the roof of the car and took the tent. He drove off, looking for water, himself, something he'd lost and had no idea how to find again. Mom quit her job and moved to the only province they hadn't been to together. I was at UBC too—studying linguistics and looking for order. We'd both emerged from a long dark stretch. I was back in school after dropping out of the Emily Carr Institute of Art and Design, after discovering I hated art school. I'd been waiting to go since I was seven.

We'd both spun out and were settling now, enjoying our minds. So we walked and pointed things out to each other.

"Walter Benjamin says the art of storytelling is reaching its end," she said. "It's because the epic side of truth, wisdom, is dying out."

"People threw cigarette butts into petrol barrels," I told her, "because they were stamped 'empty.'"

"What happened?"

"Boom."

"Look," she said. "This flower." Yellow shots in the dark wood.

"It's like a marsh-marigold." We held the marsh-marigold in our minds.

"Boom," Mom said. I could hear the sweep of them against the side of the canoe, Dad in the back with a paddle. I could feel the steel culvert under my seven-year-old bum, water tugging their stems when a beaver slid through, holding its breath, waiting for me to leave.

"You used to pick me marsh-marigolds," Mom said. I smiled. I could still see them wilting on the kitchen table while she hummed Paul Simon or Judy Collins and I sat on my feet, with crayons, drawing.

"Yes, they always died."

"The epic side of the marsh-marigold hasn't died out," she said.

The most beautiful thing about a marsh-marigold is the space around it. The trick of painting is putting the right amount of dark beside the right amount of light. Light is nothing if it isn't offset by darkness. It's obvious why so many of us love Rembrandt, Vermeer. Those of us who once believed in Jesus still lean toward Isaiah. Brightness is mere emptiness if it isn't situated in negative space, contrast. Though we wish it weren't so, we love Van Gogh, Edvard Munch, Frida Kahlo more because of the darkness in their lives. It makes their paintings shine. Marsh-marigolds shoot up out of swamp water. Swamp lanterns emerge out of winter, dark ground.

I've been resisting this as a painter: my preoccupation with light and beauty. A lot of painters feel pressure these days—to make something new, to purge the Wordsworth from their desire. I feel pressure to reject beauty, to paint for the sake of the paint, to stop asking people to make meaning out of what I'm representing and, of course, to stop representing altogether. I feel pressured not to paint, as though painting itself were antiquated, out of vogue, unnecessary. I feel pressure to be Marina Abramović, to perform instead of paint. I feel pressure to be Diana Thorneycroft, Jana Sterbak, or Damien Hirst—to unsettle instead of soothe. But the truth is

I want to take your hand and put it under a hen's wing.

I want to say: *loveliness, look, it's here*. It's hidden in calen-
dula, broken teeth,

the woman who told me God stops the rain for her: *I say
look Lord,*

I'm tired of the rain. I feel obligated to cut a cow in half, holler
hell. I should. But every time I'm flooded, I'm flooded
with splendour.

I want to paint the way I love Vancouver, the way it seeps
through me,

the fling of water from spokes, the wash of winter on
Skytrain windows,

the underbelly of eagles, the undersides of frogs, leaves.

I paint because I'm looking for the ground, a sturdy place to position what's spinning in me, my life. I'm looking for an antidote to disarray, the substance of hope. And it seems that's out of vogue too.

Mom tugged me into the bushes. "It has quite the smell," she told me. And then she did something she rarely does. She lied. "It's glorious. Breathe deeply," she said. I did. I bent and pulled as much swamp lantern into my lungs as I could. The flower attracts flies by smelling like dead meat. We laughed hard, tumbled back onto the path.

"Crap, Mom," I said, "you lied."

She grinned. "I'm learning the world." We laughed again. Then walked in silence, hands in our mittens, our mittens in each other's hands.

Two years ago my sister had a stillborn baby—a week before the baby was due.

Just before the baby died, I'd written something in a notebook about due dates. About how odd the phrasing is, like returning a book to the library. Library books don't belong to you. They are something you enjoy and have to give back. They're on loan. I wrote something about due dates being more like expiry dates.

I was painting when my sister called. I was painting a yellow door. I think it was yellow. The hallway was dark.

"We're in the hospital," my sister said. She told me the baby was dead. "I baked cookies in the morning. Now we're waiting. Her name is Keira Jo." The mundane always sits beside the cataclysmic, uninvited. I put my brush down.

"I'm drugged to the gills," she told me. I thought of Saskatchewan, Manitoba, Lake Superior stretched out between us. Her in Ottawa. Me in Vancouver. Connected by a thin line, our voices reaching each other by bouncing in the dark.

Half a year ago I hit an artistic wall. I had just finished a series of seven paintings of my bedroom window at different times of day because I was trying to paint my way into another country, Australia. I was homesick for Canada and I wanted to transform my homesickness into acceptance of my new landscape. I thought painting my window would help me see where I was living, love it more. I pushed out ideas about imitating and failing at being Monet. I thought of his huge studio overlooking the Rouen. I thought of him painting the same building simultaneously on different canvases with different light. I was looking for the ground but when I was done I was tired. The ground hadn't shifted. The place I was in hadn't changed. I hadn't changed. Things had just become more complicated. Home was still far away.

And so I decided to paint what I couldn't see. I tried to look at the world differently. I pushed myself to paint things that were no longer physical or tangible to me. I attempted to paint memories. I decided to let myself miss home.

It began well enough. I painted rain on my parents' roof. How it felt to be seven under that roof, a roof that now both exists and doesn't. I wrote a poem to title the painting. I thought about Eadward Muybridge's horse, the photographs he took to prove that the horse spends a split second off the ground when galloping. I wanted to figure out why it didn't matter to me that the horse was off the ground.

Eadward Muybridge captured motion by making it still, I wrote,

and so I am painting rain on my parents' roof. Some things
cannot be silenced. A running horse is never still, rain
is always landing. My parents were always moving away
from each other. What, exactly, do we do when we paint?
Are we cartographers of memory, are we painting ourselves
freeze-frame, documenting what we wanted, one thought
so still it is impossible? Lately I have been wondering
what we lose when the people we love stop loving each other.

The second painting was Vancouver. Wet Vancouver. Shining
Vancouver. Puddles, green, cedar, and Skytrain. I painted the rain I
had been longing for. I wrote about Mary Pratt, rain on windows. And
I thought about the constellation of moles on my father's back as he
stoked the kiln deep into the night, fireflies, sparks. This poem, this
painting, was about alchemy. *Artists*, I wrote,

take the sorrow of abandoned houses,
unvisited graves; they take snow-peas and joy and confusion
and bend them into a new substance. Artists make windows
out of dusk and shallow water. *Look*, I want to tell you, *look
how Mary makes preparation for plum jam.* She translates
a freckled pear, offers us poems to recite in the dark, verses
to comfort us when we are confined by solitude.

And then I tried to paint swamp lanterns in Green Timbers Park.
Since my mother had tugged me into them, I've spent years loving them
more. They are lanterns that remind me of, guide me, home. I did the
preliminary sketches and I thought I was on the right track.

But the painting failed. When I tried to paint swamp lanterns, I
discovered I was excavating sorrow.

Keira Jo died in December. My oma died three months later. I was pregnant for the three months that spanned their funerals. Some stories, some bodies, carry more than they can handle. I had terrible morning sickness between the funerals. My mother had called it "amendment," my pregnancy. It was also an accident. I wore my sister's sweater, the one she had worn over the bump that was Keira Jo. And then my amendment died too.

One thing made me feel better. Swamp lanterns. Beauty assuages us. The words on Oma's grave explain her position in the world: *I will sing*. Keira Jo's has the words Mom offered my sister: *may heaven be brighter for the light we lost*. While the adults were saying goodbye to Keira Jo's body, her three-year-old brother climbed chairs looking for light switches. Turning the lights on and off, saying "light, light, light."

We wanted to give Keira Jo somewhere to stand, a position in the world, even if it was myth. We wanted something to be warm after all that incubation, that waiting. We wanted light.

There was nothing wrong with Keira Jo. That was what the tests said. Of course, there was something wrong. She was dead. But her organs were perfect. Her hands were perfect. Her lips were perfect. The toque covered dark black hair. Keira Jo's toque was the same colour as the swamp lanterns—the toque she was buried in but didn't need. The toque was for us.

I took the crib apart in the middle of the night while my sister slept. I kept dropping bolts on the floor. I'm sure my sister wasn't asleep. Every time a bolt landed the stillness was punctuated. My sister stayed in her room to give me peace. I pulled the crib apart by myself to give her peace. The next day we packed the clothes up together. There was no need for peace. I sat on the floor and she sat in the rocking chair and we wept and folded tiny shirts and socks and put them into bags. We stopped trying to be strong. "I wanted her," my sister said. "I wanted her so badly."

It was -20°C the day she was buried. The snow shone. It was brutally cold. The people in the funeral parlour asked us if we didn't want to do the service inside. "No," my sister said. She wanted to be whipped by the wind. We all did. We each held a red rose in our red hands. We imagined the little body in the casket, white and dead. Our roses froze. Our hands froze. Our hands were red. Our ears were red. The warmest thing that day was my brother's hand in mine. We had to imagine what we couldn't bear—that she would be frozen in that little yellow toque by the time we went to bed.

I made silk shopping bags out of the quilt I had sewn for Keira Jo. I told my sister I hoped we might make something useful out of our sorrow. I wanted alchemy. My sister didn't need alchemy. She removed the handles. She put pillows in them. She turned them into something beautiful and unnecessary.

That's art. Beauty might not be necessary, but we need it.

For nearly six months I have been unable to paint. My failed swamp lanterns have cast a shadow beside me in my studio. Not shining. Failing. Today I figured out how to paint them. I could paint them only by not painting them at all. I didn't need to paint swamp lanterns. I needed to offset sorrow, peel the emptiness from a tiny coffin. I needed to pull off an impossible stunt—to make someone who doesn't exist outlast us all. I needed to get acquainted with the epic side of truth. I understand now why I paint, why I draw. I make art to find something so that I can lose it. I do it because the strongest things

> are the weakest things, the flammable words, the ache
> for God, immortality. I can make a thousand suns
> without igniting anything. You know what canvas is—
> it's proof, proof that one person wants to be heard,
> proof that some things should last forever, that love
> should be recorded, that beauty is urgent.

Painting translates the intangible into the corporeal. It is physical, geographic. It's the alchemy of taking the space between memory, abstraction, and the present and pressing up against it, the electricity of it, with the body. I can comfort my sister with a brush, my wrist. I can return to my crayons on the kitchen table. I can locate what I cannot comprehend but want to. I can go home.

What I do when I paint is not about legacy or innovation. It's stabs in the dark that are worthwhile. It's about burying a yellow toque, picking a marsh-marigold that doesn't exist. I paint, in fact, to come to grips with love.

JESSICA HIEMSTRA is a visual artist and writer who lives in Toronto, steps from High Park. She has exhibited internationally and has two full-length collections of poetry, *Apologetic for Joy* (Goose Lane Editions, 2011) and *Self Portrait Without a Bicycle* (Biblioasis, 2012). She has won a number of Canadian awards for her writing. She exists virtually at jessicahiemstra.com.

Delivery

CARRIE SNYDER

IT WAS THE WINTER of my fourth pregnancy. Snowbanks piled higher than a child's head. We were renovating our kitchen, and for the months of December, January, and February, we camped in a taped-off portion of our main floor. We amused ourselves by melting cheese atop a variety of edibles in a borrowed toaster oven. We washed dishes in the bathtub upstairs. Dust was everywhere. Life was cramped, contained inside one warm room where the children and I spent most days.

I took to walking, evenings. Every night, swaddled in my brown maternity coat, I walked around our neighbourhood, always following the same route. I walked no matter the weather. I came to anticipate small landmarks along the way. The little tree that had refused to drop its dead leaves. The motion-sensor porch light that flared, each time, in recognition of my passage. Once, I walked in a blizzard, struggling through thigh-high banks. Once, I let myself fall backward into fresh snow on our front lawn, thinking I would make a snow angel. The effect was less charming than imagined, much colder, much wetter, much harder to heave upright again; this was not the flavour of metaphor I was seeking.

Our baby was due on the first day of spring. But we marched past the date, and the snow refused to melt, and the baby's head refused to drop. I had never been late before, yet here I was, dilated and ripe and stalled in pre-labour contractions that brought nothing but gas. My midwives explained that multiple pregnancies had changed my body, weakened muscles, and that therefore this baby was floating freely in an expanse of warm amniotic fluid, its head nowhere near my cervix.

As the days ticked by in slow motion, as the midwives fastened elastic belts around my rotundity to keep the baby in position, as I sought out acupuncture and swallowed herbal tinctures and spent hours on my hands and knees practising yoga, I began to doubt that anything would ever change. Don't believe there's no drama in stasis; there is, it's just invisible, interior: "I understand why they call it 'delivery,'" I told my husband.

Within the small drama can be seen the shape of the larger story. This fourth and final pregnancy would end as my others had: in the birth of a live, healthy baby. But what I am leaving out is all of the disturbance surrounding us, the heavy sadness that etched our larger families' lives during this time. Cancer and death. The dissolution of a long and troubled marriage. I am leaving out how much I wanted this pregnancy to be a symbol of change, not just of birth, but of rebirth. How much I wanted the arrival of this child to mark the end to a difficult year.

Our fourth child pierced our lives like a green shoot through dry earth. That is what I wanted to believe, the story I longed to spin.

Our fourth child was conceived on Canada Day, after midnight. The tent was brand new, pitched on grass beside my brother and sister-in-law's farmhouse. Our hair was smoky from the campfire; we were tipsy. Our conversation had ranged broad and deep, and we had agreed to one last drink, and then one more. Zipped into our expansive quarters, my husband and I were glad to be together; we did not take this for granted. Our three children, ages six, four, and twenty-two months, breathed peacefully on the other side of the thin nylon wall separating our room from theirs.

It was a good night.

Good nights come no matter what surrounds them. What surrounded this one was a steady march through disturbing emotions, unwelcome and inescapable. In April, my parents had moved to separate locations, their marriage come completely undone. The family house had been emptied and sold. It had proven difficult for my mother to find an apartment of her own—difficult for her to rent, given no current employment and the legal uncertainty of her marriage status. This was shocking, and as we sat filling out routine but impossible forms in the anonymous dining room of an apartment we'd hoped she could rent, I tasted her fear, her shame and rage and powerlessness, and my own powerlessness to temper her emotions, to reassure or comfort her.

It was just a hint of the aftershocks to come.

Quite apart from this, my husband's family was lost in its own crisis. April had been a dark month. My mother-in-law called to confirm terrible news: multiple tumours found in my father-in-law's brain. Skin cancer had been diagnosed six years earlier, treated, and considered beaten; but cancer had returned to him.

I stood in our bedroom, the phone to my ear, saying, "He's lived through so many health scares. He's like a cat with nine lives."

And my mother-in-law said, "I think he's used them all up this time, Carrie. I really do."

I could not believe her. All I could manage were platitudes. I didn't know how to give anything else. I didn't know what to say. I thought blind faith was in order. I thought by expressing optimism I was doing my best. But, no, I was doing the only thing that I could manage. I was plugging my ears. Blind faith is a form of refusal, a way to reject the fears and emotions of others, to prevent others from sharing what you cannot bear to carry. *Don't go there.*

It was how I felt after we'd left the apartment that would not be my mother's after all, and she held out her hands to me, watching them shake in amazed horror. "I can't stop them," she said. "Look. I'm broken."

"You're not broken." (*You can't be.*)

"It can't get worse," my husband and I told each other as we staggered into summer. What sweet relief to tilt in lawn chairs around a fire, to reminisce with my brother and his wife, to laugh, to say yes to another drink, and, finally, floating on gin and tonic contentment, to fall into bed with my husband. Maybe this was my attempt at a fix.

Several weeks later, I figured out that we'd started something, the two of us. My husband and I were quietly elated. It seemed, it really did, that this pregnancy had to be symbolic, it had to be a sign. I can't even tell you how much I wanted it to mean *everything*. To fix *everything*.

We carried our secret around, waiting for the right moment to share the news with our families, pausing, hesitating, almost saying and then quickly pulling back. When we finally broke the news, the moment seemed almost anticlimactic, lost in the clutter, another half-baked hope.

I can recall no special details from our conversations with our parents, nothing apparently worth remembering.

I'm not sure my father-in-law even acknowledged the pregnancy, caught as he was inside a landscape of loss. In photographs taken on our visits that summer and fall, his eyes are distant, vacant, focused on an interior story that is hidden from the rest of us. I think that he was losing his connection with the future. What meaning could an unborn grandchild have for a man who wouldn't live to see his present grandchildren grow and age?

Whatever my own expectations, I was soon reminded that being pregnant is a literal state. Rather than feeling ripe with symbolism, I was done in by the first trimester's all too real physical assertions. Its meaning was the nausea, the debilitating exhaustion, the late afternoon collapse with children crawling atop me, the breasts aching, the anxiety, the usual. When a friend, pregnant at the same time, miscarried, I could not resolve the discordances. Suddenly, this accidental pregnancy seemed at best a risky enterprise, at worst an out-of-tune proclamation, an inappropriate celebration.

I started doing something a little bit odd, in retrospect. I hid my pregnancy from people who didn't know. Not deliberately, but by omission. I couldn't possibly tell you why. All I know is that I let people wonder at the flowy shirts and dumpy figure — is she?

When you are with child, you are filled, also, with vulnerability. You count the days and the weeks, and at each passing milestone you think, *okay, now I will not be afraid. Now I will stop worrying.* At fourteen weeks, the embryo becomes officially a fetus. Risk of miscarriage drops. At twenty-four weeks, or so, the fetus is considered medically viable outside of the womb. But barely. The closer you get to your due date, the more attention you pay to the signs of life inside. If you haven't felt the baby move for a little while, you drink a glass of juice and pray the sugar gets it kicking. At any point, the body might behave in some unexpected and treasonous way. You are vigilant for subtle signs of distress. When does it begin to dawn on you — or is it something you must relearn again and again? — that there is no point at which the worrying stops. No test that can be taken to relieve the mind.

At Thanksgiving, my father-in-law told his family he knew his life was over. He waited until we had put the children to bed, and then asked his own children, two sons and a daughter, and me, to sit with him at the table. That was really all he had to say: he knew his life was over, and he wanted us to go on living ours. His breathing was laboured. He asked, also, that we pray, if we were so inclined, for him to live to see another Robbie Burns day. We all knew that would be a long shot. And though I am of the praying persuasion, I couldn't bring myself to make the petition. Waiting for him to die was not something I could bear ask God to prolong. I understood how cruel and selfish it was to feel that way, but I couldn't stop myself from feeling it, and worse, from acting on my feelings — again, acting by omission. (A pattern? I'm only seeing it now, as I write this reflection.)

The waiting. The waiting seemed the hardest part.

It came to me that it was like waiting on birth. Death was as inevitable and mysterious. Even for the dying, who knew when it might come?

We visited two weeks later. I kept myself busy with the care of the children, busy with the knowledge that I was pregnant, busy with setting the table and clearing the dishes and "helping." I could hardly bear going into the parlour, where a hospital bed had been set up for my father-in-law, who was now unable to rise without help. I am ashamed to say I could not bring myself to say goodbye properly. The most I could manage was to meet his eyes from across the room, to attempt through mine to say to him, *I'm sorry you are suffering. This is awful.*

Two days after we left he passed away. It happened to be Halloween, and we were costuming the children for trick-or-treating when the call came. Communicating almost wordlessly, my husband and I reset our plans; he took the children out while I stayed home to pack and let family and friends know what was happening. We broke the news to our children post-trick-or-treating, and left immediately on the five-hour journey.

We drove through eerie, clouded darkness. We shared the Halloween treats as a bedtime snack. We talked about him. We said to each other, "We will never forget this night." And we haven't.

We were, in some way that is difficult to confess, filled with relief. To know the outcome. To know the end of the story.

Of course, that is all illusion. *Endings.* We none of us can know what will happen in the aftermath. We none of us can guess the effects, the ripples that pool outward and spread and rock our lives, and change us.

The funeral was filled with the remembered personality of my father-in-law, who had in life been an outsized character, difficult, gregarious, rule-breaking, attention-grabbing, someone who could effortlessly charm a room of strangers to laughter with a perfectly timed and outrageous toast. My husband, the eldest son, spoke honestly and movingly of the agonies and joys of having such a parent. In the packed church, ringing with the wail of the pipes, my father-in-law seemed present, and loved and remembered for who he was, completely.

But the funeral also marked another agonizing footnote in my parents' ongoing separation. The acrimony was so deep that even a funeral could not bring them together in the same room. This was a shock to discover. And with it came the recognition—almost unbelievable to me—that there was no solution that would *fix this*.

How I wanted to fix everything. No. How I demanded it. How I insisted that everything could be fixed!

My husband coped well with the loss of his father. It seemed. But in the hollow of winter his silences dug longer and deeper. He is not a man given to self-expression and I failed to notice, except to become irritated by it. We were sitting at our displaced dining-room table over a cheese melt in late February when I provoked him to speak, for heaven's sake, and he began to cry. The air in the room changed instantly, charged with raw emotion. It felt dire, like we might not recover from this moment.

Breakdown. In a partner it is disconcerting to say the least—infuriating, terrifying. I'm not sure my sympathies were great. I was in a panic. How could we fix this latest trouble, sudden and uncalled for? (As if any trouble is ever called for.) Later that night, after the children were in bed, I went for my customary walk. I asked, did I have the strength to pull us through whatever this was? I passed the little tree with its dead leaves that fluttered and rattled in the wind, and I let my tears leak. Not sobs, just dampness. I really loved that little tree: one solitary bush that had refused to drop its desiccated foliage.

What did it mean? What was the music of its dead leaves saying to me?

I thought, that winter, that the little tree was reminding me to be patient, to be faithful and watchful. It came to me that the tree would be there, with leaves or bare, whether or not I stopped to notice it. But I had stopped to notice it, night after night. I had walked past it until it had become apparent to me, and then I couldn't not notice it. But I see, in reflection, what I couldn't see then—that the little tree was also a representation of refusal, of holding on to something past its season.

No wonder it brought me such strange comfort. I saw its defiant beauty. There were so many things I didn't want to say goodbye to.

We are all, at all times, waiting for something to happen—not always for the profound, often for the mundane, but we are waiting. That long and solitary winter, I was waiting for everything to get better: waiting for light, for health, for birth, for reconciliation. I was holding tight to how I thought things should be.

We want to be agents in our own lives. We are impatient, and we are reluctant. We fear being at the mercy of forces and circumstances larger than ourselves.

Our fourth child, our last, was born at the tail end of March, ten days late, and in a breathtaking hurry when he came. "He brought spring," we sang as the snowbanks retreated and the sun stayed up late.

And it was strange. His birth did mark the literal arrival of springtime that particular year. There was something powerful about adopting the symbolism, something irresistible, something essentially unfair. Because his birth wasn't really more than itself, and didn't need to be. Many of the troubles in our lives were yet to get worse before they got better, despite this baby being born. It wasn't like a magic wand had been waved. It wasn't like we could spin the facts into a tidy ending. But that was our instinct, nevertheless. It is still my instinct, as I struggle to tell this story.

I'd wished for that pregnancy to have an aura about it—of what, precisely, I can't say. Of hope, probably. Instead, I spent many moments during those months worried and guilt-ridden and anxious and trying to avoid my fears. What if I lost this precious vulnerable growing life? How could I bear it? What would it mean? So much expectation balanced on top of a process that needed no more.

And then he was born. Joy! Bliss! Everything I'd imagined his birth would be—for about three hours or so. Because birth pushes out hemorrhoids and the afterpains get worse with each subsequent pregnancy and the baby is so terrifyingly tiny and when will the milk come in and why am I crying softly and gazing out the window and scaring my children and the bleeding won't stop and we're headed to the hospital and Jesus Christ my parents *still* can't be in the same room together, not even to meet their grandchild?

Ah. Green shoots through dry earth. They're beautiful. God, they are gorgeous. The snow melts. God, it's wondrous. Friends bring meals. Bless them. Milk flows. Blessed life. But, oh, green shoots wither. Frost kills. Friends part. Milk dries up. Blessed life.

Even in harshest winter we may find music in a little tree that holds its dead leaves. And one day we'll notice the dead leaves have fallen. The meaning will come to us, even if it is not the meaning we'd anticipated or hoped for, even if the meaning changes as we change.

I'll forget this again, and need to be reminded: there is only ever the illusion of conclusion, of ending.

We hold because we grieve. We grieve because we love. And we wait in the possibility of love without grief. We wait as best we can.

CARRIE SNYDER was born in Hamilton, Ontario, and grew up in Ohio, Nicaragua, and southern Ontario. Her first book, *Hair Hat*, was nominated for the Danuta Gleed Award for short fiction. Her second book, *The Juliet Stories*, was a finalist for the 2012 Governor General's Literary Award for fiction. She lives in Waterloo, Ontario, with her husband and four children, and blogs as Obscure CanLit Mama.

Acknowledgments

WE WOULD LIKE TO thank all of our writers, who made this book possible with their lives, their wisdom, and their work.

With thanks to friends, new and old, for believing in this book at key moments: Caroline Andrews. Stephanie Bolster. Fiona Tinwei Lam. Laura Hunse. Janine Hamming. Kim Jernigan. Gail Marlene Schwartz. Susan Scott. Lisa Pasold. Chris Tarry. Jasmina Odor. And, of course, our families. To Jonathan, for the innumerable ways you have made this book possible, and for living with me at the heart of the story all the way through: thank you. And, to all the Martins and DeMoors (extended, hyphenated, etc.) who have believed in and supported this project (and me) along the way: my love and my thanks. Thanks to the Kuyvenhovens, the Hiemstras, and especially the Dierolf family. Rachel and Frederick, you show me all the time how to live honestly and hopefully inside of the unexpected. Yannick is still showing me how to turn the lights on and Hedda is the most beautiful bundle of courage I've ever had the grace and privilege to hold.

With thanks for publishing our essays in the first place: *The Malahat Review* and *The New Quarterly*.

With thanks to our writers whose words we've borrowed for section headings — Sadiqa de Meijer, Kevin Bray, Lisa Martin-DeMoor, and Carrie Snyder.

And, not the least, with thanks for taking a risk on this little book — and so many more — in an uncertain time: Ruth Linka and TouchWood Editions.

And, to those of you who wanted to write something but weren't able, to those who had the courage to submit something that wasn't included, to everyone with a story like this to tell: this book is for you.

A loosely linked series of anthologies about the twenty-first-century family, *How to Expect What You're Not Expecting*, *Somebody's Child*, *Nobody's Mother*, and *Nobody's Father* are essay collections that deal with childbirth, childlessness, and adoption. Together, these four books challenge readers to re-examine traditional definitions of parenthood and family.